A.N.T.S.

A.N.T.S.

The American National Transportation System

Keith R. Felix

iUniverse, Inc.
Bloomington

A.N.T.S.
The American National Transportation System

iUniverse books may be ordered through booksellers or by contacting:

iUniverse
1663 Liberty Drive
Bloomington, IN 47403
www.iuniverse.com
1-800-Authors (1-800-288-4677)

ISBN: 978-1-4759-1018-6 (sc)
ISBN: 978-1-4759-1019-3 (ebk)

Printed in the United States of America

iUniverse rev. date: 04/28/2012

CONTENTS

Part III – Funding Methods, Project Organization, Support

Part IV – Opinions & Origin of A.N.T.S.

INTRODUCTION

We have a lot of problems facing our country today and the root cause for many of these problems is Unemployment! If we can solve this problem then some of the other issues facing our country might be easier to resolve. But how do we do this?

I believe it is time to take bold actions that will help reduce the unemployment rate to a much lower level and at the same time make an investment in our country. This is a proposal for creation of a new transportation system in America. Build this and it will be used.

This story is about a project that will help invigorate our manufacturing industries for decades, stir innovation, encourage students to seek education in mathematics and engineering and strengthen our ability to compete and trade in the international marketplace. This is a project where it will not make sense to outsource the work to other countries. I believe that this project in conjunction with a commitment to addressing our infrastructure problems will be a revival for our manufacturing industries and our economy.

We are the greatest nation on earth and the main reason is we have the greatest foundation for a free government ever devised; the United States Constitution.

Second, we have the greatest defense forces in the world today; a brave and dedicated voluntary force of men and women serving our country!

Third, we have a population that on whole is the most generous in the world. Americans are willing to come to the aid of a neighbor in need, whether it is across the street or on the other side of the world.

We need to improve our economy because it is a large part of being the greatest nation on earth. Without a vibrant domestic economy that includes a strong manufacturing base that can create any goods needed, a nation may not remain a great nation for long.

One example is the Soviet Union; they did not have a system of government like we do, but at one time they had one of the strongest armed forces in the world. But what they did not have was a strong economy that could produce domestic goods and services as well as military equipment for their forces. Their leaders chose only the latter.

History has several examples of nations that went the same way. The founding fathers of our country provided a map for us to create a great nation with many individual rights and freedoms. Along with that comes a responsibility by our leaders to follow the constitution and the will of the people. We the people have a responsibility to elect those leaders who will protect those freedoms, and follow the will of the people.

CHAPTER 1

AMERICA SEEKS SOLUTIONS TO UNEMPLOYMENT PROBLEM

Since the summer of 2011, I have had a lot of spare time. I started off watching a lot more sports on the cable and local channels. Eventually, I began watching news and business programs. In the morning I usually split my viewing time between three or four cable business channels, and then in the afternoon I would mix in some of the news shows. I would finish off the day with a combination of news and business programs and some prime time shows in the evening. It seems that many of the networks and cable channels lean one way or another politically speaking, so I watch various news channels so that I can get a wide range of opinions and comment on the news of the day. Whenever I needed a break I would watch game shows and for awhile, I got hooked on watching The Price is Right.

Time and time again, commentators and guests on these business and news programs similarly expressed their frustrations about the number of unemployed, even about what work will be available for the returning service men and women, and most of these people asked basically the same question, as for example, "What can be done to create more construction and manufacturing jobs"? How can we get a sustained economy going? What is the catalyst?

After awhile, it felt like they were talking to me personally. They did not directly state, if you have an answer or idea, send it in. But, I reasoned they must be implying that they wanted a solution from someone. So I went from there and started thinking about the core problem of the economy and after a short time, the answer seemed fairly simple to

1

me. It affects millions of people; a lack of opportunity to find and get a good job.

I also remember that on a few of these programs, I heard some people affirm that there are jobs out there, and that all these unemployed people need do is get out there and look for one! Well, to some extent I would agree with that sentiment as there are some jobs out there. I know that if you have special skills that someone is looking for you may find that job; say in information technology, or in the health care field. Additionally, they usually followed up with the recommendation that you get some training if you do not have the skills employers are seeking. That is all they need do. It was not mentioned, that once you get the training, many find out that another requirement for the position is experience. It can be very frustrating.

Some say that if you are unemployed, all you need to do is start your own business! I do not totally agree with that statement, but I do agree that every citizen has the right to pursue his or her dreams and either succeed or fail. You cannot say that about every country, can you? The truth is that many people have come here from other countries, and many still dream about coming to America, just for the opportunity to live in freedom and start their own business.

In reality though, I think that for any trade or service in a given area, there is a finite amount of potential customers for sales or services, before saturation occurs. If you are only competing against a reasonable number; let the best business win. This is how it should be in a free market driven economy, right. My point is that for everyone in our economy who is out of work, starting their own business is not a realistic solution to the unemployment problem.

Many people have their own opinion on why we have such a huge unemployment problem in our country and who is to blame for it. I do too, but at this point, I am not looking at someone to blame. What is important for us to recognize and agree on, is that there is a major unemployment and under employed problem in America and find a solution to it.

The problem has been building for decades and I believe it is directly related to the loss of jobs in our manufacturing industries. We have tried to compensate for this problem by spending billions of dollars on short term projects that in most cases, employ only a few for a short time. On an annual basis, we have to spend billions of dollars on support programs to keep the millions of people without a job sustained and that is only at a minimal level. Of course without tax revenue coming in our budget deficit continues to grow. Last but not least is that the value of our dollar continues to shrink. Even if you are one of the fortunate ones who have money, you must occasionally be concerned that you will need more money just to stay even; why, because every year the value of our dollar seems to buy less and less.

As for me, I kept thinking about the unemployment problem and eventually, came up with what I believe is a solution to the problem. I reasoned that we could fix a large portion of the unemployment problem for decades if we had a project in America, like the one I have described here. I also determined that a key part of getting this project accepted and underway is knowing how it will be paid for, or funded. You may disagree, but I believe the project would be most beneficial without a majority of the funds coming from our government treasury. For one reason, we cannot keep adding to America's budget deficit; it needs to be reduced. For another, we need to get this project going as soon as we can and if the federal government is controlling all aspects of this project, it would be decades before it is completed and thus many of its benefits lost.

I believe the American National Transportation System (ANTS) is that solution to the unemployment problem we have in America, and this is my attempt to convince you that it is too.

I am a private citizen who has spent about the last 40 years analyzing and designing systems in the world of Information Technology. I am not degreed nor do I claim any particular expertise in the areas of construction, engineering, or manufacturing.

To keep this story short, I have provided the current links to the information I reference, rather than add the material to this book.

Unfortunately, some internet links change over time and no longer point directly to the original source. However, by using key words related to the information in any particular section, you can usually obtain similar sites or the same sources I used for my research.

The first part describes the system and its components; the next part covers the cost, impacts, and benefits of the ANTS project, followed by a section that provides three methods to fund the project and an organizational plan to manage it. Then least important, I added a section containing my thoughts and opinions on the unemployment problem and some of its' causes; it might be interesting to see if you and I agree on any of the reasons I have listed. Then if you are curious or interested, I have a brief piece on how this idea came to me.

Finally, I believe most Americans are concerned in one way or another with the situation we are in. You may be unemployed, or related to someone who is, or just know of someone who needs a job or a good job. Maybe, you have plenty of money but are concerned about the value of the dollar, especially, if you are retired and on fixed income. Perhaps, you have just returned home from serving our country and are looking for a job. No matter what your reason, if you want to take some action to reverse the course our country is currently on, please read on.

THE AMERICAN
NATIONAL TRANSPORTATION SYSTEM

This American National Transportation System (ANTS) project is an idea for a new addition to our nation's current transportation system.

ANTS is designed to create new transportation channels, stretching from coast to coast and border to border. Its main structure is a single platform above the surface, which from a distance would resemble a very long highway overpass. On this platform, the three major components of the system; energy, communication, and people, will be transported over routes connected to one another that form a national grid.

The project is designed to create good long term jobs in the private sector, with numbers in the range of 1.5 to 2 million workers directly and indirectly associated with the project, year over year. Its further purpose is to provide the backbone for a true National Energy Grid with overall lower cost energy, access to additional transportation channels and secure communication links that will serve our countries needs for many decades.

The American National Transportation System is an economical and ecologically friendly system. I believe this project will help make our country more competitive in the international marketplace, spur innovation and new manufacturing and make our country more secure.

OVERVIEW OF A.N.T.S

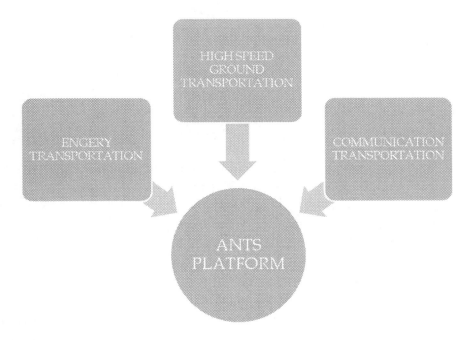

Figure 1.1

There are three components to ANTS and they all sit on top of what I call the ANTS platform. This platform is a continuous structure and sits up off the ground along the entire routes (see proposed routes, Fig. 2.1).

The ANTS platform is off the ground for efficiency purposes and to be less of an impact to the environment, existing systems (roads, farms, railroads, sensitive areas), and for safety reasons.

It is a combination of three major systems. My reasoning is that it would be more economical and ecologically friendly to have all three on one platform rather than individually constructed.

The American National Transportation System will be scalable as future modifications to the system would be easier to accommodate than if these systems were separate. Examples would be: installing additional electric power lines or communication cables along the route; modifying slots (switching tracks for the rail component from standard rail to new surface transportation technologies). The latter could be done to one slot or set of tracks while still operating on the other. What would it look like? I think that from a distance the platform would look much like a very long overpass, simple but effective.

The vertical spacing between the ground surface to the bottom of the platform is 12 - 16 feet, to accomodate all interstate & military requirements.

Figure 1.2

Note: Illustration meant to resemble an overpass as can be seen in our interstate highway system.

CHAPTER 2

America's National Transportation Routes

Where does it go?

This is a map showing potential American National Transportation System (ANTS) routes. Many of these routes could parallel our existing Interstate Highway's.

Figure 2.1

To view a map of our NATIONAL HIGHWAY SYSTEM-see website; http://www.fhwa.dot.gov/planning/nhs/.

I developed the proposed routes (fig. 2.1) after studying maps from the Department's of Transportation, Energy, and Interior that covered the interstate highway system, location of current sources of energy producers and proposed renewable energy sites and where the population centers are geographically located.

I do not believe that the selection of routes will take long to complete and base that on the fact that it has already been done for the highway system. I believe the American National Transportation System (ANTS) routes could parallel much of our Interstate Highway system. You do not need to excavate and level a path to install ANTS like you do for a highway or traditional track for a railroad. You bypass that work because ANTS is above the surface and uses variable lengths of the support pillars to level the platform. This creates less of an impact on the environment too! The only extreme excavation might occur if you wanted to tunnel through a mountain rather than go around it.

As you may know, most interstate highways are directional and whether it is two lanes, four lanes or more, traffic flows one way in those lanes; just like ANTS. Normally, there is also a separate interstate highway going the other direction too; true? Often, you will see a sizable distance between these two directional highways that goes for miles and miles. I am sure that in many places, engineers can determine how best to utilize that space to fit ANTS in between the highways, or alongside one of them.

Furthermore, in these spaces and areas along our interstate highway system, I would also assume that many issues related to rights of way (ROW) or imminent domain, have already been resolved. These comingled systems would be true transportation corridors.

INITIAL ROUTES

It might be a political decision as to which routes on the system start construction first. My thought is that we would establish a continental connection first for the Energy and Communications Grid, and fulfill some of the transportation needs of the most populous corridors by developing the East, West, and transcontinental routes as per below. Simultaneous development of these five routes would greatly reduce unemployment.

Figure 2.2

Once the initial routes are complete (fig. 2.2), population centers around the country would be connected. The National Energy Grid would be available to supplement some of the highest population centers for extended lengths of time, along with providing power to some rural areas. Additionally, new sources of energy obtained for example from renewable resources, could soon be tapped.

Planning and defining the ANTS routes is a key part of the project. Once this is complete, then other businesses can plan, design, and begin ramping up labor and material resources for their part of the project. For one example; you would need to know where the ANTS routes are going to be located, before planning where to construct new wind and solar farms, so that the renewable energy can be efficiently collected and transmitted for use by the ANTS energy grid. Those businesses handling the installation and operation of the electrical energy and communication components need to know where the routes will be, so they can do capacity and network planning and where any energy stations or regeneration facilities (discussed in chapter 3) might be needed.

Also, states and cities need to know where the routes will be so they can plan the location of high speed ground transportation ports (HST Ports, as a short name), and intra state connections to the main American National Transportation System routes.

NEXT ROUTES:

Some of these additional routes, perhaps the next five, could be in the planning, design and even construction phases, once the initial routes were underway. Again, it is very important to establish and define the routes early so that businesses can plan for new factories, materials, and indirect support industries that the new routes will need in the manufacturing and implementation of the ANTS routes, including platforms, bridges, and operating equipment.

Additionally, intra state connections to the main ANTS routes will be desired and needed. States, cities and businesses will need to plan, design, and fund their projects too.

Prior to completing transcontinental connectivity, those routes that are ready for passenger traffic between two High Speed Transportation Port's or terminals, could begin service.

Design is underway in California, Florida, and other states for various types of high speed ground transportation (HST) and most if not all are probably designed to use existing surfaced based tracks, dual purpose tracks. Now would be a good time to revisit these plans.

Reminder: Routes (hopefully at least five to start) will be under construction at the same time, and multiple crews will be working on each route; just like was done when the first Trans-Continental rail road was constructed. This means many, many jobs! Also, with the construction underway on multiple routes, any lessons learned from this initial effort would be applied to subsequent routes.

PLATFORM

The ANTS platform is the foundation of the system. It rests on pillars in the same manner as does a highway overpass (fig. 1.2). The platform is continuous from one point to another and is logically connected at terminals at the beginning of one route through to the end of the route, with stations or terminals along the way.

I envision that these platforms or pieces of the platform can be constructed to various specifications and created in factories all over the country; then assembled and finished, on site. At one end of the platform there will be extrusion pieces that are designed to fit or plug into the end of next platform section to make the platform easier to align and enhance the structures strength. An illustration that shows how the platforms connect is available in appendix A.

The platform is comprised of four major parts. The first is the surface structure and this sits on top of the pillars or supports all along the routes. The pillars would conform to the interstate vertical requirements so that all existing military and federal clearance requirements would be met. I would envision that a standard height would be assigned, perhaps 10, 12, or 14 feet, and when necessary the height of the platform and pillars would be gradually increased along the route, so that the proper clearance at the obstacle; crossing over an interstate highway for example, would be met.

Resting on top of the platform at each side for the entire length of the route is what I will refer to as the utility structure, or box. Inside the box on one side of the platform is where the fully insulated electrical energy cables are stored, and on the other side of the platform in its own box, is where the communication cables and fiber optics are stored. Racks or other structures would be located inside of these utility boxes to keep the insulated cables separated from each other. Engineers would design these parts to maximize capacity, and for efficient identification, installation and maintenance purposes. For example, starting inside the box, at the bottom of the wall and moving up the rack on the back wall of the box is cable number one. You would want and need to know that is cable number one, whether it is 50 or 150 miles down the platform.

Additionally, the platform structure can be designed and configured to carry cables underneath its' surface area too. They would only be visible from underneath the platform. I have provided further ideas on this configuration in chapter 3, where the energy component of the system is discussed in more detail.

In between these box type structures is where the slots for the ground transportation areas are located. Around the world there are different types of high speed ground transportation systems in use today. One is often referred to as High Speed Rail (HSR), and they have wheels that ride on tracks just like most Americans might think of when the term rail is used. Although, these high speed trains go really fast!

Another high speed ground transportation system I often reference is called, MAGLEV. This stands for magnetic levitation and these are high speed ground vehicles/coaches that do not ride on tracks but use magnets and electricity to hover above the surface and are guided down a pathway, or slot. Because these two types of systems are so different, I refer to slots when discussing them rather than just tracks. I also reference the equipment that operates on these slots as High Speed Transport Systems (HST). I remember that when I started doing research on this component of the system, how amazed I was; even startled, at how advanced some of these high speed ground transportation systems are and how many countries around the world use them today, with the exception of the United States.

Another key point in the American National Transportation System design is that traffic is one way, just like our interstate highways. This means that at several High Speed Ground Transport (HST) terminals (just like airports where passengers board and de-board), facilities would be required to turn or switch the High Speed Ground Transport around to the other slot heading in the opposite direction, if a return of the same equipment was needed. Of course in theory, a HST, could go all around the system and return to its starting point.

There are tradeoffs with each type of High Speed Ground Transportation (HST) systems and ANTS is designed to accommodate both types. From my study of these systems, the High Speed Rail (HSR) system would be most often used around all the routes and MAGLEV for point to point or shorter routes with minimal inclines. Technologies in these systems are constantly improving, so I could be incorrect on this point.

I have designed two types of platforms called; Type A and Type B, to accommodate different levels of passenger traffic. There are high level views of the platforms surface area in appendix a.

There are several reasons the platform is off the ground but to me, safety is number one on the list! Other reasons are highlighted in chapter 3; the discussion of the individual transportation (energy, communications, and passenger) components of the system.

Platform Details and Cost Estimates

There are two versions of the platform; Type A and Type B, and the major difference between the two types of platform is the width of the platform and this is due to the number of slots in each platform. Slots are the areas where the high speed ground transportation equipment operates. I have been using 60 feet as a standard length of either platform. I realize that other lengths will be needed to handle unique situations.

Engineers would design the platform pieces, including the supports or pillars, so that they can be manufactured at several facilities. This will allow more jobs to be created at either existing or new manufacturing plants. Although not mandatory, I expect some manufacturing facilities that create unique platform pieces will be located in a close proximity to a route for timely delivery to the construction site.

Resting on top of each side of the platform is the utility enclosure or box. One side contains the electric energy cables and the opposite side of the platform is the utility enclosure or box that contains the fiber optic lines and communication cables.

These utility boxes could be part of the platform design or if necessary, separate structures that are attached to the platform. Inside these boxes would be racks or other design structures that will allow for the maximum number of cables to be carried along each route. Each side would stand five feet high, two feet wide and would also serve as a wind break for the High Speed Ground Transportation (HST) slots between each side. I am confident that engineers will probably design a better configuration than this one I propose. It just needs to be accessible for authorized personnel to install and maintain the energy and communication contents in each utility box.

The platform sections will interconnect. Each section of the platform rests on pillars where some pillars might be prefabricated, and where necessary contain mechanisms between the pillars and the platform to handle any fault area concerns.

PLATFORM VERSION: TYPE A

The Type A platform has three slots for High Speed Transports (HST), either the High Speed Rail or MAG LEV systems.

PLATFORM TYPE A—Dimensions

Three slots or track areas and each slot is 11 feet in width.

SLOT 1 Directional =======→
SLOT 2 Service Slot/and alternate slot
SLOT 3 Directional ←======

There is one utility area or utility box on each side. The width of each box area is 2 feet. The height is 5 feet.

WIDTH OF THE TYPE A PLATFORM IS 37 FEET. LENGTH IS 60 FEET.

TYPE A would typically be used for those parts of a long route that do not serve large populations along the route. An example of this would be the route from Seattle, Washington (SEA) to Minneapolis, Minnesota (MSP) (see fig. 2.3). The TYPE A platform would be 37 feet in width. Although, either Type could be used, Type A, might be more economical to construct on this route, as it has only 3 slots or lanes.

I estimate the cost to manufacture and construct 500 miles of Type A Platform to be in the range of: 2.5 Billion to 3.6 Billion dollars. This does not include any design, engineering or bridging costs. See the data I used for estimating the low and high costs for the platform and supports in appendix a.

PLATFORM TYPE A - USE ON ROUTE SEA to MSP
PLATFORM TYPE B - USE ON ROUTE LAX to LAX

Figure 2.3

PLATFORM VERSION: TYPE B

The TYPE B platform would typically be used for those parts of the system that serve large populations along the route. The TYPE B section of the platform is 50 feet in width. An example of this would be the route from Los Angeles, California (LAX) to Las Vegas, Nevada (LAS), reference map routes (fig. 2.3).

The Type B platform has four directional slots for High Speed Transports (HST), assuming two for the High Speed Rail and two slots for MAG LEV systems. Each Slot is 11 feet in width. Of course, when necessary, one slot can be designated to be a service slot or lane.

PLATFORM TYPE B—Dimensions

Three slots or track areas and each is 11 feet in width.

SLOT 1 Directional =======→
SLOT 2 Directional ←======
SLOT 3 Directional =======→
SLOT 4 Directional ←======

There is one utility area or utility box on each side. The width of each box area is 2 feet. The height is 5 feet.

WIDTH OF THE TYPE B PLATFORM IS 50 FEET. LENGTH IS 60 FEET.

I estimate the cost to manufacture and construct 500 miles of Platform Type B to be in the range of: 3.8 Billion to 5.5 Billion dollars. This does not include any design, engineering or bridging costs. See the data I used for estimating the low and high costs for the platform and supports in appendix a.

CHAPTER 3

System Components—Energy

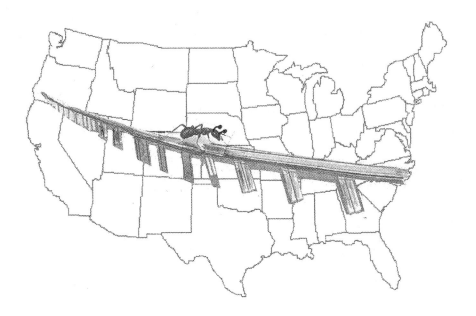

This part of the system can be the basis for a true national energy grid! It will accept electrical energy from all sources. This would include existing power generators (your local utility) and transmission systems, along with renewable energy sources that would hopefully, be located close to where they are most abundant or available; Solar, Wind, Geo Thermal, Hydro, and others. The American National Transportation System (ANTS) would then be capable of distributing this energy all over the country via this new grid in a seamless manner.

This energy would then be sold wherever needed to its customers, just like utilities currently do today and any fees generated would be collected by the systems operator and any applicable taxes would be paid to local, state, and federal governments as is done today.

The following information is provided to highlight our countries current electrical transmission methods and capabilities, the types of electrical current that can be transmitted, and a brief history of electricity's beginnings in our country.

I believe this background information is necessary to understand how the Energy Component of the American National Transportation System (ANTS) can play a large role in our energy needs going forward.

BACKGROUND ON EXISTING SOURCES OF ENERGY

Electrical energy or electricity is a product created or generated from other sources; coal, gas, oil, nuclear, etc., and through renewable resources such as hydro (dams), wind and solar, wave action and geo thermal. According to information on the Department of Energy Information, website, http://www1.eere.energy.gov/water/pdfs/51315.pdf, hydropower or electricity produced from dams is the oldest source of power. As of 2010, it produced around 6-7% of all the electricity generated in the United States. It is still the largest producer of energy from all renewable resources. The history of power generation from water is interesting and I have placed some additional information obtained from the Department of Energy, on this source in appendix b.

In the United States today, coal is the fuel used to generate the largest of amount of electrical power created; 57 percent. We have an abundance of coal reserves in our country, but it has some environmental problems; hopefully, these issues can soon be resolved with new and improved technologies. However, no matter what source of fuel is used to generate the electrical energy, once it is created it must be used. Very little electricity can be saved. Where is it saved? It can be found in the batteries that we use to power our flashlights, radios, cars powered by electricity, and other devices powered by batteries. We have not yet developed the ability to store mass amounts of electricity for later use!

In America, we are very fortunate to have consistent power available at the switch, ready to use, on demand. Of course there are outages from time to time due to weather issues or when demand exceeds supply, and other reasons too. Through my research I have learned that it is no accident or by magic, that we have such a reliable electrical supply. A lot of dedicated people have invested money and energy into making this happen over the last several decades. There has been much effort put into building new high power transmission lines all over the country so that companies can share available electricity where and when it is needed.

I do not look forward to paying my electric bill every month, especially, in the summer, but I now understand a little more about what is involved behind the scenes, to ensure electricity is there when needed.

It is easy to take for granted that electricity will always be there, so long as the bills are paid. To me, it is kind of like insurance, lawyers, and a few other things that you do not think much about until you do not have it, and you need it. I now realize that there are not a bunch of giant electrical cords laid out all over the country that utilities just plug into as needed. I have also learned that one limitation of the use of renewable resources is that, in some cases where it is most advantageous to use the wind, the sun, the waves, or the heat from the earth, to generate electricity, there is a problem getting the electricity, from the source to the market!

Our country needs all the power it can generate, and we need to be able to obtain electrical power and deliver it to anywhere in the country, so that cities have plenty of it and so new factories and manufacturing facilities have consistent power to run their businesses and power their equipment; again, anywhere, on our part of the continent. I believe that the energy component of the American National Transportation System can be a large part of the solution to America's energy needs.

EXPANDING THE CURRENT ELECTRICAL GRID

This is information that supports the energy component of the American National Transportation System (ANTS). It describes the current electrical transmission system that we depend on when there are outages in one part of our country and how that energy is replaced.

According to an article published on October 30, 2009, on the government internet site called Energy in Brief, website, "http://www.eia.gov/energy_in_brief/power_grid.cfm", there is no "national" power grid. The article states that the "national" grid is actually three separate power grids. They are somewhat geographically aligned and are known as the Eastern, Western, and the Texas grid, with tie lines or links connecting them. In addition to these three grids in the United States, they also mentioned that large areas in Canada are fully integrated or linked to the Eastern and Western grids, and that parts of Mexico have some connectivity to the Texas and Western power grids.

There is an organization called the NERC (North American Electric Reliability Corporation) that is responsible for aspects of this international electricity system. According to information on its website, www.nerc.com, its mission is to ensure the reliability of the North American bulk power system, which I take to mean the "national" energy grid. The electric reliability organization (ERO) is certified by the United States Department of Energy's Federal Energy Regulatory Commission, to establish and enforce reliability standards for the bulk power system. Canada has similar certification commissions for the ERO in that country, and I assume Mexico does too. It is a self-regulating organization that relies on its diverse and expert members to ensure compliance, although, it is subject to audit by the United States Federal Energy Regulatory Commission. In the section called "Understanding the Grid", it notes that the NERC is serving some 334 million people and had coverage responsibilities for over 211,000 miles of high-voltage transmission lines.

After reviewing many articles on the NERC's and other subject related websites you can get a sense of what some of the difficulties are in expanding the current "national" grid. An expansion of the grid would normally mean constructing additional transmission lines within one of the grids or from one of the grids (Eastern, Western, or the Texas) to another. The purpose for expanding transmission systems is to provide additional or new power to communities or regions, and even to replace old transmission systems.

The expansion of the electric transmission system is expensive. Because of this, companies will sometimes form a joint venture to share in its cost. One example of this is occurring in Indiana today, by the Duke Energy and American Electric Power companies. They have a 50-50 partnership on this one project and are going to build an extra high voltage (EHV) transmission system using 765 kilovolt (kV) lines. The system will be constructed between electrical stations that are close to the cities of Kokomo and Evansville, Indiana. That is approximately a distance of 240 miles, with an expected price tag of $1 billion dollars.

Expansions are costly in both dollars and time and in the end, we all pay for them. Power companies try to maximize their efforts by transmitting as much electricity as is safe to do over these new transmission lines. One term you often see when reviewing the information on the new power transmission lines is Extra High Voltage (EHV). The highest that I have come across for long distance transmission so far, is described on the American Electric Power company website, and it is a 765kV line. Other load carrying lines often mentioned are 500kV, and 345kV. Some of the considerations that go into the line selection process are the available right of way (ROW), height and structure of the transmission towers, distance of the transmission line, sea level, terrain, typical weather for the area, type of insulation needed or not for the wire; type of conductors, and determining if the line will be a composite or not; I always thought that all those lines were made of copper.

Types of electrical current

One other consideration is the type of current in the line. It will be either alternating current (AC) or direct current (DC). Alternating current is what is used most of the time in the United States. We use it in our homes and it is in the transmission lines for the most part.

Transformers are a key piece of equipment in the transmission of electrical energy using alternating current; they increase or *step-up* voltage in the transmission line so the line can carry more power and then are used to lower or *step-down* the voltage at the off point so it can be used in our homes.

Direct current is most familiar in our use of batteries. It is my understanding that direct current is used somewhat more in other countries than in the United States for transmitting power over longer distances.

Undersea lines (transmission lines that are submerged under water) also use direct current most of the time. Apparently, DC power is easier to control than AC but the problem with DC power is that it is expensive to convert to AC, and we use alternating current in most everything we power in our homes, factories, and offices.

Direct current uses equipment called a *rectifier* to convert alternating current into the direct current form for transmission and then uses an *inverter* to transform direct current to alternating current. This does not seem to me that it would be expensive, however, it apparently is and often a decision point on whether to use it or not for the selection of the current being transmitted.

For long distance transmission of bulk electrical energy it seems that a High Voltage Direct Current (HVDC), for example, a 500 kilovolt high capacity line, is favored by some, but then there still is the conversion process to be considered. From my research, it appears that the use of DC current to transmit electrical energy in the United States maybe increasing soon. I also read that there are European companies working on creating systems that will resolve issues in the DC to AC conversion more efficiently, and I hope that some American companies are working on this too. The debate in America over which form of electrical current to use in transmitting electrical energy; either alternating current (AC) or direct current (DC) is interesting and started in the late 1800's, between some famous inventors and entrepreneurs.

THE EARLIEST USE OF ELECTRICITY IN AMERICA

Since the beginning of our country there have been many Americans that have made important discoveries and advances in the field of electricity; however, two come to my mind most often. They are Benjamin Franklin, and Thomas Edison.

Benjamin Franklin was a many faceted individual. Most Americans probably are aware that he was one of our countries founding fathers and played a major role in the establishment of our country. He was also an inventor and scientist and many refer to him as "The Man Who Tamed Lightning". Even in today's world, I would assume Benjamin Franklin's name would often come up when discussing important discoveries and inventors who had a major impact in the area of electrical sciences. I am sure many people are aware of his famous experiment with kite's to see if they would attract lightning when flown during a storm. He was assisted by his son in this experiment, and of course, the kite did attract the lightning which led to the development of the lightning rod. This invention has saved lives and an unknown amount of property damage. Prior to this invention, lightning often struck people's homes and buildings and set them afire. But once you correctly located a lightning rod by your property and grounded it, the lightning would go after the rod and the energy was transferred to the ground, instead of striking your house. The lightning rod is still in use today.

Thomas Edison developed the first electrical power transmission network in the United States and pushed for its use across the country. It used direct current to transmit the electrical energy. However, George Westinghouse had seen alternating current (AC) systems in Europe and decided they should be used in the United States too, rather than direct current. The debate was on. Eventually George Westinghouse hired Nikola Tesla, who at the time was the technical leader of a group that was working on their version of an AC transmission process, and the competition grew into something more than a friendly rivalry.

There was a lot of money involved too. For one, Thomas Edison held a lot of patents related to the direct current process and obviously stood to gain financially if direct current were to become widely used. There were also personal issues involved in the debate. Nikola Tesla had at one time worked for Thomas Edison. He reportedly left his employ with Edison for a number of reasons; primarily though, because Thomas Edison did not accept Tesla's preference for using alternating current instead of direct current. There is a lot more to this interesting story and there is plenty of information available in books or on the internet about it. If you search the web for it, just look for "battle of the currents" or "War of the Currents".

PROCESS OVERVIEW—NEW OVERHEAD TRANSMISSION SYSTEMS

After an energy company determines there is a need for additional power and decides to construct a new transmission line, then the planning process begins. It seems to me that one of the most difficult issues to overcome in the whole process is finding a site for the right of way

(ROW), where the transmission lines and towers will be constructed. The ROW is usually 150 to 300 feet wide. Getting approval of the ROW can be expensive and time consuming. It involves getting permits and approvals from the state, cities and towns, private land owners, and the Environment Protection Agency (EPA). This phase of the project is further compounded when multiple states are involved.

In some cases the right of way (ROW) area has to be cleared for the entire distance of the transmission line. Installation cost varies due to the terrain and location of the site. This phase of the project can take a long time. If you think about it, most of us do not mind a transmission line being installed somewhere, so long as it is far away from our homes and our cities and cannot be seen!

Once the planning process is completed and the design is finished, then the construction can get underway. Of course, this is just a simplified description of what it takes to get an electric transmission system implemented. If interested in additional details on this process, I would suggest you review the websites of several power companies. For example, American Electric Power (AEP), website www.aep.com/about/transmission/transmissionqa.aspx provides information on its own expansion efforts, costs, methodology, and easy to understand terminology in a section that addresses "transmission questions", including the pro's and con's of direct current and alternating current power transmissions. The information also addresses the use of undersea energy cables, which must be used in some cases and is currently being looked at by other communities, as an alternative to high voltage line systems strung over the land.

Finally, once the system is installed, you have the ongoing maintenance of the right of way, keeping trees and other vegetation clear of the wires and the structures, and repairing any equipment that goes awry due to time and the elements.

ALTERNATIVES TO OVERHEAD TRANSMISSION LINES

There are some areas in the country that refuse to accept any new overhead transmission lines and utilities have had to find other methods to provide power. And then, there are other situations where the power lines cannot be constructed on high transmission towers, because there is no land, as happens when supplying power from a mainland to an island, or across most large bodies of water.

One alternative to overhead transmission systems that is sometimes used is to bury the high powered transmission cables. This is similar to what is done today with lower voltage lines in many neighborhoods. However, this is not always a solution. Besides the cost, there is sometimes a problem due to an interaction between the current and the buried cable which at times can alter the voltage in the line to undesired levels. When this occurs, it can be costly to locate and repair the problem. Issues with buried cables also arise when they are accidently dug up, too!

High power transmission lines that are placed underwater are often called undersea or submarine cables. They are in use today, all around the world. A common example would be in supplying energy from a mainland source to an island or from one island to another, such as is used in the great state of Hawaii.

Recently, submarine cables have been a solution to overcoming environmental and architectural concerns in several locations in the United States too. People just do not want to see the high powered transmission lines! However, just like the lines that are buried under the ground, they have problems too. First, you need the water; oceans, rivers, bays, and lakes and they need to be in the right place to be useful.

For example, I am most familiar with the Missouri and Mississippi rivers and if you look at a map of the United States, they mainly flow from the North to the South. There are not a lot of rivers in the Midwest that flow East and West. However, I can understand that when the options are limited, you use what you have available. I can see that in some situations, using the submarine cables would be an alternative or even a requirement, to using overhead High Power Transmission lines.

There has also been some concern from environmental groups that laying a cable in some rivers or lake beds might cause the sediment to be stirred up and pollute the water. According to the Office of Electricity Delivery & Energy Reliability under the website ENERGY.GOV, nearly all long distance submarine cables use direct current because the loss of energy on the line is less than alternating current and the power is easier to control. As previously mentioned, converting the DC power to AC power is expensive.

WILL ANTS REPLACE EXISTING ENERGY TRANSMISSIONS SYSTEMS?

I am not claiming ANTS can resolve all problems related to the delivery of electrical energy, however, I do think that it can eliminate the need for a lot of new and visible transmission structure systems and become either an independent energy grid, or a supplemental part of the current energy bulk network, perhaps, serving the three individual energy grids as their reserve or backup system.

Additionally, it will provide new areas of the country, especially remote areas, with the ability to hook up to ANTS and sell energy, and or, have access to energy. When using the same amount of electrical energy transmitted as a base of comparison, I believe the relative cost of materials and installation would be much lower carrying the electrical lines inside of the ANTS structure and below it; rather than stringing up the cables on high tower structures (fig. 3.1).

THE ANTS ELECTRICAL GRID

Energy transmitted through ANTS will be able to go through or next to metropolitan areas and provide additional power to those areas as needed, and at a modest cost compared to burying lines underground, underwater, or attempting to install new high power transmission lines. Plus, because of its design and the concealed cables, it overcomes those who object to new transmission systems due to environmental or aesthetic concerns.

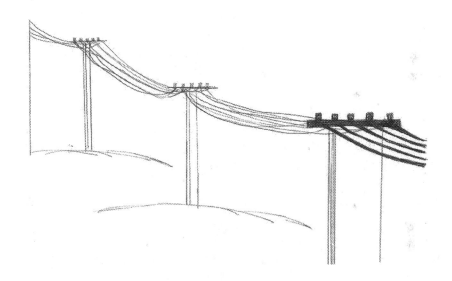

Figure 3.1

According to information on the Department of Energy Website, and depending on the cable size, and type of transmission current, *generated electricity* is good for up to 300 miles before it starts to dissipate. As previously mentioned, one problem with renewable energy is getting it collected and sent to where it can be used to generate electricity. Therefore, I believe we will need some new facilities created along the ANTS Routes to support the energy transmission system.

I envision that there would be collection facilities or energy stations where energy would be delivered (see fig. 3.2) no matter what the source; wind, solar, hydro, or power from utilities. These energy collection stations would receive the energy over transmission lines and know what type of current, AC or DC, it was processing. Then the station would generate the electrical energy in either a DC or AC current and transfer the power to transmission lines within or below the ANTS structure. Once the ANTS routes are fully implemented across the country, then they should be accessible via a transmission line for any energy farm to connect to.

The regeneration facilities would be strategically placed along the system to correlate with the distance energy within ANTS can be transmitted without losing too much power. These sites might be in the same location as the previously described energy stations in some cases. These facilities would monitor the transmission lines on ANTS and extract energy off the system to run electric turbines that would generate new electricity. This energy would then be put back onto ANTS and sent along in either AC or DC current. Additionally, excess power could be sold and transferred to local power utilities directly or indirectly to energy stations to power manufacturing facilities.

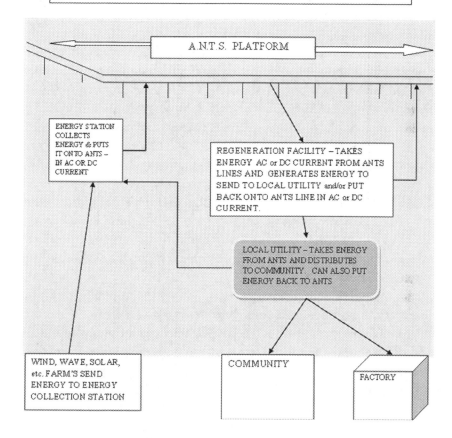

ANTS ENERGY STATION & REGENERATION PROCESSES

A.N.T.S. PLATFORM

ENERGY STATION COLLECTS ENERGY & PUTS IT ONTO ANTS – IN AC OR DC CURRENT

REGENERATION FACILITY – TAKES ENERGY AC or DC CURRENT FROM ANTS LINES AND GENERATES ENERGY TO SEND TO LOCAL UTILITY and/or PUT BACK ONTO ANTS LINE IN AC or DC CURRENT.

LOCAL UTILITY – TAKES ENERGY FROM ANTS AND DISTRIBUTES TO COMMUNITY. CAN ALSO PUT ENERGY BACK TO ANTS

WIND, WAVE, SOLAR, etc. FARM'S SEND ENERGY TO ENERGY COLLECTION STATION

COMMUNITY

FACTORY

Figure 3.2

As part of the National Energy Grid, operators and control systems would divert any needed power to other systems connected to ANTS for that purpose. That could mean supporting one of the three existing grids (East, West, or Texas Grids) on a scheduled basis and/or emergency basis to thwart any outages in those systems. This would create a true national energy grid across the United States, and provide the energy to support new manufacturing facilities, and keep our energy costs low.

Electrical Systems designers and electrical engineers would determine the number and line capacities of the electrical cables that could be safely contained within each box. Also, they would know how to space any cables carried underneath the platform and what insulation would be needed. For example, those giant cables that are carried on the overhead transmission lines (765kV) might be used by ANTS, but only under the platform surface. If they are too large then a lower configuration using the 500kV, 345kV, or other size might be a better fit. As previously discussed, these cables carry a lot of energy and depending on size and atmospheric conditions, can create some noise. If these large capacity cable sizes can be safely used under the platform, perhaps they would have to be further incased in plastic piping to reduce the noise, at least in populated areas.

The electrical designers and engineers would also determine what type of current, alternating or direct, to use. If necessary, they would create the hardware and software to control the conversions between them and how to route the energy. For example, for those renewable energy resources that plug into the system (see fig. 3.2) they would know what is needed to receive the energy from the source, and in what current, and how to manage it.

As we all know, most renewable resources are not a continuous stream of energy. If the wind does not blow or the sun does not shine much one day, or the flow of water through the dam is not very strong, then, there will likely be volatility in the amount of energy produced, at that time and place. To get an idea of where the renewable resources are most prevalent by type, see the maps on http://www1.eere.energy.gov/maps_data/renewable_resources.html".

Again, when the American National Transportation System is fully implemented, one huge benefit will be the ability to collect, generate and distribute locally supplied energy to customers that are located just about anywhere else in the country, or continent.

On August 23, 2011, an earthquake struck the East coast and several Nuclear Facilities in that region had to be turned off for weeks as a safety precaution. Fortunately, existing energy systems handled the loss of these power generators. The energy transmission component of ANTS will further enhance the National Energy Grids capabilities for handling emergencies, no matter where they occur in our country.

We currently have a pretty stable supply of electrical power for many of the dense population centers in our cities, towns, and factories. ANTS will enhance and support these current systems and bring additional energy to where it is needed. It will also be able to deliver electrical energy to expand or build new cities, towns and manufacturing facilities all across our part of the continent. We need to reduce congestion in some metropolitan areas, and we do have room to expand in our country. ANTS can ensure we have the necessary electrical power available for these new areas and help keep energy costs at a reasonable price so we can compete in the international marketplace.

I believe the Energy component is a very important segment of the American National Transportation System. Ensuring adequate supplies of power are available all across our country and at an economical cost is good for the consumer and the manufacturer. The American National Transportation System can be a key part of our nation's goal to become energy independent.

SYSTEM COMPONENTS—COMMUNICATION

An additional use of the American National Transportation System will be to contain communication transmission cables and fiber optics, across and up and down our part of the continent. This would provide additional capacity, redundancy, and distribution options for high speed land line based communications.

Today, there are many communication systems in the United States and around the world. These could be public or private networks and might generally be identified as being wireless, or wired; land lines, long haul land lines, voice communication lines, data, fiber optic, cable, satellite, and networks with a combination of transmission types. The ANTS communication facilities could supplement or enhance most of the existing government and privately owned networks in use today, and even support the creation of new networks.

For examples of what areas of the country these existing networks cover, visit individual network sites you may be familiar with, or you might check out this website, www.telecomramblings.com/network-maps (ref. *Long haul network headlines*) as it has links to maps that show many of the domestic and international long line, cable, and fiber optic communication networks.

In the following (fig. 3.3), I roughly outlined the coverage area of just one network over the continent. I also showed a representation of a few of the land lines that leave the United States and link up to networks on other islands and continents. The land based networks are connected one to another, by means of under water or submarine communication transmission cables. These underwater cables have been around for quite awhile as some of the initial large scale submarine lines were used to transmit telegraph signals between continents. I am assuming that many of the new era cables are now fiber optic type transmission lines.

The American National Transportation System will support the concept of Cloud Computing, by providing additional volume and high speed transmission links. It will provide more opportunities for consumers, educational facilities and businesses to access and interact with others in the cloud communities no matter where they live within the continental United States. This also means access to cloud systems all around the world.

A.N.T.S.	COMMUNICATION NETWORK

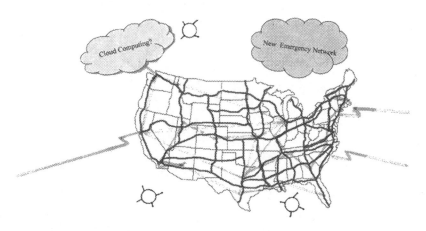

Figure 3.3

There is a lot of money involved in both the wired and wireless telecommunications industry around the world. If you are interested in the size and scale of these revenues, you can do an internet search on the key words 'telecommunications industry' and 'related revenues'. There are many reports available.

Businesses and government entities primarily use land lines for data center processing, large volume transmissions, and for speed and security reasons. The additional facilities provided through the American National Transportation System (ANTS) could be used by current network owners to expand their services, or for redundancy purposes. Much of a networks business is providing communications facilities to other businesses. And, a responsibility of operating any business, especially, a communications related business is having redundancy; the capability to switch to a backup system when your primary system or network is having problems.

Today, it is expensive to expand land based portions of a network. If you examine the network routes (fig. 3.3) I previously mentioned, you would notice that many parallel our interstate highway system. This is no accident as communication lines and cables are often laid along side of our highways. They are also strung up on the high wire transmission systems used by electrical companies to transmit electrical energy. That means those desiring to expand their networks or communication grid, face the same constraints in some cases as do the electrical energy businesses encounter, when wanting to expand their electrical services capabilities.

ANTS will provide the ability to easily install and store new communication lines and fiber optics in the protective cover of the box on top of the platform. It would be more economical for any land line based communications related company, to expand on ANTS, rather than trenching and burying these communication lines along highways or strung up with the electrical cables, all around the country. Plus, it is more environmentally friendly. Additionally, more people could be served in that the ANTS platform will cover the continent and not just the high density population centers. This will provide people and businesses living and operating their businesses in remote or rural areas with access to high speed connectivity and communications.

The Federal Communications Commission (FCC) says that in this century, communications technology and services are critical to our country's economic success, contributing to our economic growth, education, and health care services, to name just a few. I believe that the American National Transportation System will make a positive contribution towards achieving these goals.

The ANTS communication network will provide the capacity and access for more Americans to have real time access and participation in online; meetings, collaborative efforts on scientific and medical research. It will also provide increased educational opportunities for students all across the continent. ANTS will help keep communication transmission costs low too!

Teams will be able to efficiently work together, on all sorts of projects. Many types of resources can link up in a real time mode; industry, university, government and business, to solve problems and for virtual hands on education, with fast reliable service at a lower cost. We have technologies that provide online meetings and web services available right now. They connect people for live conferences and meetings. With the extended coverage area of the ANTS communications network, it will expand the availability and communication type capabilities to more users across the continent. Plus it could be used as a redundant or backup system to television, cable and satellite networks that currently cover the United States.

Additionally, with a network this widely dispersed, even a new communication carrier could create a network. Also, any fees or leasing expenses currently collected by government entities on existing networks would apply to ANTS, and any fees due would be collected by the federal and state treasuries. I believe the ability to easily install and carry new cables and fiber optics in the protective cover of the box on top of the platform, would be much cheaper and more environmentally friendly, than trenching and burying these communication lines along highways or strung up with the electrical cables, all around the country.

Similar to the energy component, ANTS will provide consumers and businesses access to high speed communications all over our country. Communication brings us closer together as a nation and this new channel will support rural areas and new population centers all over this great land with the same level of consistent speed and quality that consumers in existing population centers have come to expect and rely on.

ENHANCED WEATHER ALERTING AND EMERGENCY PREPAREDNESS

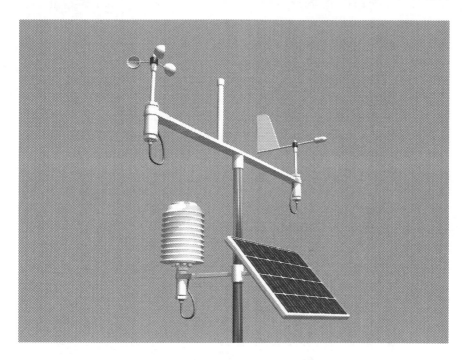

I believe an additional benefit of the American National Transportation System (ANTS) communication component will be to serve as an early detection and emergency warning system. One of the systems I was responsible for when I used to support airline operations was the weather system. At that time, I worked on computer programs that produced flight plans for the airline and I became familiar with the weather data used in that system. I did not design these particular programs but they seemed to do the job; my job was just to make them work more efficiently. Of course that was many years ago but I remember that it used data based on predictions of what the upper level data, such as wind, speed, direction and temperatures were going to be at a location a certain number of hours into the future. The program used a mapping system called Marsden Squares to plot this data against. I believe each square was a 10 by 10 degree area aligned along latitude and longitude lines. Each square had a unique number so it was possible to receive this data from a weather service provider over network communication lines, store it in a digital form and use it programmatically in the selection of flight planning routes.

Later in my career I worked with weather data in another system that focused on providing ground weather forecasts and other information to airlines and the public, at least to those that had access to our system. This weather was provided by the National Weather Service who distributed the various categories of weather data on a periodic basis. The origin of the weather data was from local airports and other locations, and some of the data was forecast in nature and someone had prepared these forecasts before distributing them. We stored this weather in our computer system and produced displays as desired by our customers. I know that back then, the local radio and television stations used much of the same data as a base for their forecasts.

Today, there are a lot more sources of weather data available and there is a lot of technology and businesses involved in gathering, analyzing, and forecasting weather data. We have several good meteorologists in my city and at times I switch from station to station to see their forecasts. It is sometimes surprising to note the variances between them on their forecasts for the amount of expected precipitation, and temperature, or where and when a storm will appear.

I still think the National Weather Service is responsible for issuing severe alert warnings. I know they have a lot more technology than they did many years ago. I believe the American National Transportation System could enhance the systems currently being used to collect weather data, in addition to airports and other locations that are still sending in weather data to the national system.

I envision that weather collection devices would be placed along the ANTS routes with close proximity to one another. This would provide a more granular look at real-time conditions and enhance the current surface weather data. This data could be collected and transmitted to the National Weather Service on a periodic basis or upon demand. Additionally, inexpensive systems could be placed along the ANTS routes to analyze the data they are collecting and based on variances from the weather usually collected, alert local or national emergency offices of potentially dangerous conditions at that specific location.

This additional information could enhance the capabilities of the emergency agencies responsible for alerting the population of possible severe weather conditions, at any time of the day or night. Using the ANTS grid for collecting, analyzing and tracking surface level weather conditions in conjunction with all the latest radar technology keeping watch in the skies could help save lives.

Additionally, the American National Transportation System communication grid could monitor seismic activity in the same manner as previously described for surface weather data collection and analysis.

System Components—Transportation

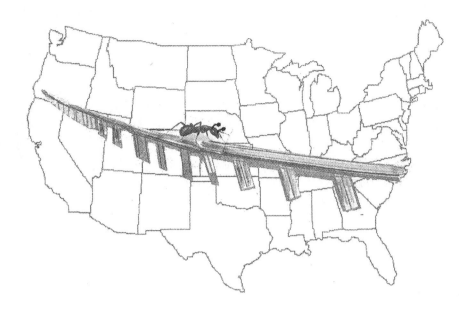

High Speed Ground Transportation (HST) for passengers is the third component of the American National Transportation System (ANTS) operating on the platform. ANTS would not transport heavy freight due to weight constraints and because freight traffic is being handled very efficiently today by traditional railroad operators. The system would probably be most beneficial on shorter city to city or regional routes; however, ANTS is a national grid and capable of supporting trips from coast to coast, and border to border, just as our interstate highway system does today. The transportation component of ANTS is simply designed to deliver people safely and efficiently, from one location to another in a very timely manner.

A key piece of the systems design is having the ANTS platform elevated above the grounds surface. This ensures that High Speed Ground Transportation Systems (HST's) can operate under almost all weather conditions. Additionally, it is much safer than conventional surfaced based ground traffic as it is free from the hazards and tragedies that current passenger rail travel encounters; such as collisions with vehicles at crossings, or encountering animals and other obstructions anywhere along or on the track.

The design of the traffic flow in the slots is directional, just like the interstate highway system and means all traffic goes in one direction or the other, but not both ways on any slot or track (reference appendix A, Platform Design Features).

All traffic on the system will be monitored by high speed ground transportation controllers at a regional level and at local levels in a similar manner as air traffic controllers do when handling aircraft between routes and at the terminals. Also, there will be service centers located along the routes that have equipment to handle any problems that might occur with the operation of high speed ground transportation systems (HST's). Finally, for redundancy purposes, on board safety systems would ensure HST operators and their equipment, know what is ahead of them on their slot or track; for example, utility workers in the area or equipment in their slots, and can then take manual or automatically take action to slow, or stop if necessary.

I must admit that when I began research for this project and did some initial searches on high speed trains; I was shocked by the results that quickly appeared on my screen. I could not believe how many nations have high speed ground transportation systems and was amazed at how long some countries have had these systems. After thinking about it, I realized that some of these countries lack of natural resources, and the related high prices for those resources necessitated alternate forms of fuel efficient and environmental friendly ground transportation for them at an earlier time, than us.

TYPES OF HIGH SPEED GROUND TRANSPORTATION

I have focused on two types of high speed ground transport systems; one is high speed rail (HSR) and the other is MAGLEV. High speed rail is most like traditional passenger train systems in that they have wheels that run on train tracks. However, these HSR's look nothing like the passenger trains I had remembered; they are now aerodynamic and very attractive machines. Of the HSR systems I have reviewed it seems most of these are powered by electricity or gas turbine engines. Cruising speeds are in the 175 to 210 miles per hour range.

Just like air carriers, High Speed Rail (HSR) carriers configure their equipment to what is needed for a particular route. They optimize the configuration based on the number of passengers per route, and where the equipment is needed next; down line or for a return trip. For example, one HSR I reviewed was setup with a seating capacity of around 600 passengers and this required about six passenger compartments and one power unit on each end of the HSR. Many HSR configurations have similar service classes too; First Class, Economy Class, and on some configurations, a separate Business Class.

MAGLEV is short for magnetic levitation and is one of the newest forms of high speed ground transportation available in the world today. These high speed ground transports levitate above the surface and move along the slots or paths by a positioning of magnets that create a magnetic force field. Once they are up to speed they do not use wheels or brakes and they do not have engines. Everything works through the manipulation of the magnetic force fields. They are capable of very high speeds and I have seen them advertised as operating in the 200 to 300 mile per hour range; some even claim they can go faster than this.

I believe they are actually in commercial use in Japan and China, and there are companies in America that are partnering with Japanese companies to try and get some of these systems in the United States. To view an illustrated and descriptive process of magnetic levitation, check out the Pennsylvania High Speed MAGLEV Project, using the TECH tab at website, http://www.maglevpa.com/tech.html.

To review additional information and get a look at High Speed Ground Transportation (HST) and MAGLEV transportation systems, search on "High Speed Rail" or "MAGLEV". Some sample websites by country:

Japan http://www.usjhsr.com/USJHSR/Welcome.html

France http://www.raileurope.com/train-faq/european-trains/tgv/index.html

China http://www.smtdc.com/en/gycf3.asp

Other related websites:

MAGLEV.NET http://www.maglev.net/

High Speed Trains http://www.ushsr.com/hsr/trains.html

We are way behind other nations in the world as regards high speed ground transportation. Put in terms of the airline transportation industry, they are in the JET age and we are still in the PROPELLER age. The good news is that by building the American National Transportation System we can quickly catch up with these other countries in the use of high speed ground transportation, that is, if we want to. I hope we do and have plenty of reasons to do so.

High speed ground transportation in the United States is way overdue. I cannot explain why it is not here! This part of the system will produce many jobs. In addition to all jobs related to the design and manufacture of the platform that will contain the slots where the high speed ground transportation operates, there are thousands of jobs directly related to the support and operation of the transportation system; high speed rail, MAG LEV, system operators and customer service positions; on board and off. Then there are the controllers who ensure that the operators of the carriers follow all rules and regulations in their operations, similar to the air traffic controller positions in terms of passenger and crew safety.

Eventually, if not already underway, we need American companies to design and build new models of high speed ground transportation systems. These may be in the form of high speed rail or MAGLEV systems that will operate on the ANTS platform and one day, perhaps compete for sales internationally. We already have business concerns in this country partnering with foreign companies to bring these high speed ground transport systems to the United States. ANTS is designed to accommodate both high speed rail (HSR) and MAGLEV operations.

New businesses, (New Carriers) would supply the equipment to transport passengers on the system in a competitive mode just like airlines do today. As with the airline passenger, the ANTS passenger would be subject to ticket fees and these taxes would go into the federal, state and local treasuries.

In addition to the direct jobs this component of ANTS will provide, there are other benefits to this project for our country.

- ANTS will provide additional transportation channels for our population.
- It will reduce some contention with land owners and problems with Right of Way issues that the current proponents of high speed surface rail have.
- ANTS is more environmentally friendly as compared with surface based high speed ground transportation.
- It will serve as a national security component in times of emergencies.

- It will provide some relief from congestion on the interstate highways, especially, in high population centers.
- It will improve railroad freight traffic by removing some passenger traffic and gradually remove the use of our nation's current rail system from being a dual purpose train network, serving both passenger and freight traffic, to primarily a freight system.

Finally, it will provide many indirect jobs that can add to the overall job numbers created through just this one part of the American National Transportation System.

DESIGN CONSIDERATIONS

A key piece of the systems design is having the ANTS platform elevated above the surface. This ensures almost all weather operating capability for the HST passenger. Additionally, it is much safer; free from the hazards and tragedies that current rail travel encounters such as collisions with vehicles at crossings, or encountering animals and other obstructions anywhere along the track. High speed ground transportation moving as fast as 180 miles per hour can be efficient and run on timely schedules if it is not hampered by railroad crossings or other potential hazards ahead of it that would be encountered if the system is surface based.

Secondly, the design of some current high speed surface rail systems routes, plow right through land areas, sometimes farms and ranches and cause angst among land owners. The ANTS High Speed Ground Transportation System is operational above ground, and much less intrusive on land owners and the environment. Hopefully, most ANTS routes will be able to follow existing interstate highway routes and in those cases where it does not, its design will not totally segregate large land areas. For example, if an ANTS route went through a grazing area, the livestock could still move around and under the platform; on a hot day, they might even like the shade from the platform. I remember seeing a piece on a television program where a farmers land was split up with the proposed path of a high speed ground transport system as the right of way went through the middle of his property. ANTS might go down that same route; however, because it is above the ground, he would still have access to his land on both sides and underneath the ANTS platform. The ANTS platform is high enough off the surface for him to get his farming equipment under the platform.

Additionally, since the ANTS platform is above the surface, there is no need to level the right of way (ROW) and permanently eliminate the environment underneath the platform. This will lessen the impact on wildlife or domesticated animals in those areas where they exist with respect to freedom to move about. In most cases, they will also not be subject to sudden impacts from high speed transportation vehicles. The design flexibility of the system should also proactively handle most situations where there is a possibility of harming an endangered species environment too, as the length of the ANTS platform can vary and hopefully a problem of this nature could be handled in the design phase for the particular route. For example, rather than destroying the habitat in the routes path, ANTS might simply be able to go over it.

Another benefit of the American National Transportation System (ANTS) is that it would serve as a National Security Component. Obviously, when there is a local or regional disaster, such as occurred with Hurricane Katrina back in August of 2005, ANTS would be available to serve in a disaster relief capacity. High speed ground transports from many of its operators could be called upon to swiftly transport and disperse a large number of people all over the country. This would reduce the congestion on highways and local services.

Transportation is big business; billions of dollars are involved! One estimate says that on average there are about 50,000 aircraft operating in our ATC system every day. Many of those are most likely privately operated; either way, that is a bunch of flights! Any disruption to the system can cost millions of dollars every day it is not working; just look what weather can do to the airline industry. While our Air Traffic Control System is world class, it is vulnerable to being shut down by those who would do our country harm, as was experienced back in September of 2001. There have been many security improvements made since then; however, today there are other concerns. Some experts are now worried about the system being compromised via a cyber attack, possibly even shut down.

The operational control of the passenger transportation portion of ANTS is of course much less complex than the Air Traffic Control system. It does not need satellite transmission capability, radar, or GPS navigational systems to know where a High Speed Ground Transportation (HST) operator is or to track its movement. The ANTS transportation component can be operated effectively without too much automation and operations could be manually controlled if necessary. In the event of a disruption to our air transportation system, ANTS, and our interstate highway system would keep America moving.

We need to do all we can to reduce CONGESTION on our highways and current rail systems. ANTS could reduce some highway traffic and would help more in some areas than others with respect to reducing the number of cars between a given city pair; for example, most urban cities in California, and Florida, a few in the Midwest, and several on the eastern third side of our country. I have seen various reports about traffic congestion problems on the television and internet (search traffic congestion) or view the CNBC special, "The Race to Rebuild America's Infrastructure or go to the Department of Transportation Website to review the various data and what it costs us in time and money.

For example, one statistic from a 2009 Department of Transportation report on Congestion sited, that we spent an extra 4.8 Billion Hours more on the road and used almost an extra 4 Billion gallons of gas dealing with congestion on our roads factoring in all sources of delay. At $3.00 a gallon that is around $12 Billion dollars worth of gasoline. With an increase in population and especially when the economy gets better, we can expect that the congestion problem on our highways will only escalate. In the aggregate, this costs all of us more than just personal money for this extra fuel. When there are delays due to congestions, the business that some companies perform, such as deliveries to stores, fuel to gas stations, and delivery of packages are delayed and that cost has to be factored in and be paid. In most cases any extra cost is probably passed on to the consumer. Lastly, there is the frustration and consternation that many of us feel when we encounter these congested areas and cannot get out of them.

Regarding freight traffic, many railroad engineers will tell you that passenger trains can be disruptive, a pain in the caboose. Passenger trains usually have priority over freight trains. As my brother, a Vietnam War Veteran by the way, who recently retired as a railroad engineer told me; many times he has had a call from his dispatcher who would tell him he was going to have to move to a siding and wait for a passenger train to come by. He explained that sometimes it might involve a couple of hours; waiting for the passenger train to come and go by, and then gearing up to get his train moved from the siding, and back onto the main tracks. Again, extra fuel spent waiting, delayed shipments to customers, and time of course is money! I mentioned my railroad engineer brother's service in Vietnam and will note that I have another brother who served in Vietnam too, because I am proud of their service. Also, as a reminder that many of the jobs that will be generated from the American National Transportation System (ANTS) project will be a good fit for our returning men and women veterans. Do you agree?

There are also safety related issues involved with the dual purpose use of surfaced based railroad tracks in some locations. In 2008, the United States Congress passed the Rail Safety Act that mandated "Positive Train Control" to be implemented on specific rail lines by the end of 2015. An overview of this is available on the Federal Railway Administrations website http://www.fra.dot.gov/rrs/pages/fp_1265.shtml. Some of the key parts of the act are intended to prevent; train-to-train collisions, derailments by enforcement of speed limits, train movements through a switch left in the wrong position, and safety issues to individual workers.

In addition to the thousands of jobs that will be directly created to support and operate the passenger transportation segment of ANTS, there will be even more that are indirectly created. For one example, part of the company in which I had most recently worked with provided information technology services for the Tourism Industry. I believe that with a national system like ANTS, many new business opportunities for employment and revenue would be created within just this industry.

The dollars involved in the tourism industry are amazing; please review the information about the potential for additional jobs in this industry, under the section "Tourism", in Chapter 4.

Around the country, there will be thousands of service type jobs needed at the High Speed Ground Transportation (HST) Ports, just as there are at airport terminals all across the nation. These will include car rentals, lodging, food service, shopping, and security jobs. Further, additional jobs might also be created, as new transportation systems within a city or state are constructed for example, to link up to the terminal or port on a High Speed Ground Transportation route.

Yes, we are way behind other nations in the world as regards building our own high speed ground transportation systems, but that is not all bad. We can take advantage of this position. The good news is that we do not have to start at the bottom of the technology barrel. We do not even have to spend billions on research and development to create the necessary technology to catch up with other countries in this industry; and we sure do not have to, nor want to reinvent the wheel.

United States companies can be created by entrepreneurs or through joint ventures and they can operate a high speed ground transportation (HST) business on ANTS, along the same model that startup airlines are currently formed. The technology and equipment exists and is available from many experienced companies, worldwide. Once we gain knowledge and experience in this industry, we can then apply American ingenuity and innovation to this equipment and become internationally competitive in this industry.

This component of the American National Transportation system not only creates JOBS and CARREERS, it creates OPPORTUNITES!

CHAPTER 4

Project Cost's

Questions

What is the cost for creating a national energy grid?

What is the cost for creating a land line communication grid?

What is the cost for creating a high speed ground transportation system?

What is the cost for creating all three at the same time on the one platform?

ANSWERS

In my opinion, common sense says it has to be much less expensive to create one platform rather than three separate systems!

Much cheaper to maintain!

Future enhancements and expansions would cost less.

Plus, it creates a smaller footprint on the environment.

The purpose of this section is to contrast the cost of the American National Transportation System (ANTS) project with the cost of not doing this project. If we do nothing, then we will probably continue to annually spend billions on programs that sustain millions of our citizen's lives at a minimal standard. In my opinion, even when the economy appears to be reviving, with a rising stock market, and the published rate of unemployment leveling off or going down; it will not be long term and robust because we do not have a large enough manufacturing base as part of our domestic economy.

Would you agree that we need to restore large numbers of people to the middle income group for the long term? For example, shrink the true rate of unemployment to between 4% and 5%? I believe the ANTS project can do just that!

Obviously, when you think about what the total cost of this project with all the proposed routes completed might cost, it seems expensive. Just thinking about all these numbers reminds me of the old saying about numbers that says, "Figures don't lie, but liars figure". I could simply supply numbers to use in a cost/benefit analysis, but I believe there is a more accurate way to analyze the costs and benefits in terms of dollars, for the initial routes.

ESTIMATE THE COST OF THE INITIAL ROUTES:

I would first get the cost estimate for the initial five routes over five years. Experts from the private and public sector need to provide these. Each route would be a different cost estimate. I have provided my own estimate for the cost of the platform by mile in appendix a; however; again, I would rely on the experts to provide that number. Then for each route, take the cost of the platform and multiply by the number of miles in that route; add in cost estimates for bridges and anything else, unique to that route. Then total all five routes and divide by five to get the cost per year.

ESTIMATE THE SAVINGS AND TAX REVENUE:

I would derive the savings or the reduction in costs by taking a percentage, perhaps in the 10% to 15% range, for example 12%, and multiply this number against the cost for the funding of all related support systems for one year; include food stamps, housing and medical costs, and unemployment. Then take this annual amount times five. Add to this the payroll taxes received from 1 to 2 million direct and indirectly related (Project ANTS) employed persons with a middle income range over five years. Do not forget to add in the employees and employer's taxes for funding Social Security (FICA) and Medicare over that same period. Take this total and divide by five to get the annual savings.

COMPARE AND CONTRAST:

With these two estimates you would be able to see and compare the projects estimated costs and benefits on an annual basis and over a five year period.

As a former project manager, I have completed and been responsible for many project estimates. It is common sense that the degree of accuracy of the estimate depends a lot on the raw numbers you use in formulating the estimate. If you or your team has experience with all the resources and costs that go into the type of project being estimated, you can develop a fairly accurate estimate. I believe reasonable estimates can be obtained for contrasting the project costs against the savings so long as we use experts from both the public and private sectors.

The following are examples of some costs previously mentioned that the American National Transportation System (ANTS) project can reduce and a few comments on the projects benefits.

Unemployment Costs

We have millions of people out of work and some say that the monthly unemployment rate is actually higher than published, as they say it does not include those people who are no longer searching for a job! It also does not include those jobs that have been eliminated over the years as in the manufacturing sector and that will not be coming back, unless something is done to actually create more manufacturing jobs. According to a Dec. 5, 2011, article on the CNNMMONEY website, "www.money.cnn.com/2011/12/05/news/economy/unemployment_benefits_extension", by Tami Luhby, $434 billion dollars has been spent on unemployment benefits over the last four years. Tax payers have contributed about $185 billion dollars of that total, and state and federal taxes on employers contributed the rest. The estimate for 2012 is $44 billion dollars.

Food Stamp Costs

The number of people receiving food stamps is at an all time high and logically, so is the cost. According to a report from the Center on Budget and Policy Priorities, the Federal Government spent about 56 Billion dollars on SNAP which is the food stamp program, in 2009. The food stamp program cost 56 billion dollars in 2010. Also, in a report, that aired on May 31, 2011, from ABC News, Huma Khan reported that, "A record number of Americans—about 14 percent—now rely on the federal government's food stamps program". Reference the SNAP Annual Summary Report, next, and you can see that as of December 1, 2011, approximately 45 million Americans were receiving Food Stamps and the total cost through that date is over 75 billion dollars. The following is a partial report from the SNAP (Supplemental Nutrition Assistance Program, formerly known as food stamp program). Database through 12/1/2011.

Fiscal Year	Average Participation in Thousands	Monthly	Total Costs in Millions of Dollars		
2011	44,712	133.84	71,812.10	3,518.78	75,330.89
2010	40,302	133.79	64,704.41	3,604.14	68,308.55
2009	33,490	125.31	50,359.92	3,275.31	53,635.22
2008	28,223	102.19	34,608.40	3,031.60	37,639.99
2007	26,316	96.18	30,373.27	2,817.26	33,190.54
2006	26,549	94.75	30,187.35	2,715.74	32,903.09
2005	25,628	92.89	28,567.88	2,504.25	31,072.13
2004	23,811	86.16	24,618.89	2,480.14	27,099.03
2003	21,250	83.94	21,404.28	2,412.01	23,816.28
2002	19,096	79.67	18,256.20	2,380.82	20,637.02
2001	17,318	74.81	15,547.39	2,242.00	17,789.39
2000	17,194	72.62	14,983.32	2,070.70	17,054.02

The ANTS project would more than put a dent into this budget buster. In addition to all the jobs that it directly and indirectly creates, there will be even more jobs created due to the "ripple effect". Just the dollars saved from removing people and families from the food stamp program, and other assistance programs could offset a lot of the costs of the ANTS project and that is if it is funded by the government. Also, the intangibles that can come with having a good job; security, piece of mind, and self-respect, contribute to a stable individual, family and community.

I believe a project like ANTS can spur innovation and new industry, just like the NASA project, and the development of the interstate highway system have done for many years.

There would be more jobs in the mechanical and engineering fields and all levels of skilled and unskilled workers would be needed. Hopefully, this will encourage more students to pursue advanced studies in the field of mathematics and engineering too!

People would have money to SPEND! I believe the current housing problem could possibly self correct. Over time, the housing industry might once again become a vibrant industry. People might also buy more cars, trucks, medical care, and even, go on vacation!

The most important benefit of this project is JOBS! We have millions of folks out of work across all job categories. This includes many service men and women who upon returning from their service to our country cannot find a decent job.

Number of Jobs—Basis for Estimation

One of the easiest numbers to throw around is the number of jobs that will be created. I have stated that the American National Transportation System could directly and indirectly generate 2 million jobs over a period of time. Someone else could just as easily say it is more like 4 million jobs, or another could say it is more like a half a million jobs. The obvious question is then, who is correct?

This is the method I used to create my estimate. First of all, I used a time frame of five years. The work that I am estimating is for designing and constructing the ANTS platform, and all the complementary pieces, including bridges and terminals (HST ports) where the platform would interconnect.

I used construction workers as my focal point for the ratio of direct to indirect workers. I did this in the same manner that the military uses when comparing the total force needed for troops. For example, one combat troop might require 5 support troops. This would not include the materials providers back home who make the war materials or the farmers and factories that supply (grow the food, package the food, and ship the food) the food the troops will eat.

My ratio for support workers to construction workers is 10 to 1. I include all the designers, surveyors, engineers, material suppliers and factory workers who manufacturer materials, and equipment, for the construction workers to use in building the platform. Then add all the back office jobs involved; accounting, information technology, and other office workers.

Note: I have not included the additional jobs that could come into the count through the ripple affect; those that supply food and lodging, medical related services, and those industries that would benefit from all the ANTS workers income. This would include those workers who produce and sell new cars and trucks, home construction and even entertainment related industries and services, where the ANTS workers might spend some of their discretionary income.

I have assigned the number of construction workers for each route at 30,000 workers. This could vary depending on the route, and in either direction. With a 10 to 1 ratio, that would come out to 300,000 workers for each route. I believe we need at least five routes under construction initially; this comes to 1.5 million workers involved with the design, and development of the five platforms, per year for five years. Further, I believe the impact from these workers labors could easily produce the ripple effect of supporting another million jobs. I have not even added in the number of workers that would be directly involved with the three components of the American National Transportation System; energy, communications, and people transportation.

IMPACTS TO EXISTING INDUSTRIES

The purpose of this section is to identify and highlight potential impacts to existing industries, businesses, and anyone that might be concerned with this project impacting them in a negative way.

Just about every new invention or idea faces objections by some that are often borne out of fear of the unknown or concern that their way of life will be impacted. I believe this is a rational feeling and there are many examples where an idea or invention has replaced a way of life.

In our history, an example of this is the horse and carriage being replaced by the automobile. Of course this occurred over a long period of time, but the automobile did replace the need for horses to pull the carriage, and did replace the carriage, and eliminated those jobs that used to build the carriages, and also reduced the need for many blacksmiths that used to shoe the horses. On the other hand, millions of jobs were created in the automobile manufacturing industry and millions of people were more mobile and millions of jobs were indirectly required for the support of the industry.

Today, the automobile industry that was originally powered by gasoline or diesel fuel is itself facing change. Due to the price of some natural resources and government mandates concerning pollution, the industry has the need to use new energy sources such as electricity and natural gas, to power its vehicles. Over the years since the automobile showed up, some negative impacts it had were on the environment; smog, pollution, and later, competition for natural resources, mainly oil. As it relates to jobs though, thousands of people now work on maximizing fuel economy for those engines that still use gasoline and diesel fuel, while reducing carbon emissions, and improving or inventing new batteries and engines to use natural gas and electricity to power our cars and trucks.

The following are some potential areas of impact I have identified and some rationale I hope will eliminate any unnecessary concerns. There are probably others too. This project's main purpose is to create jobs, but it is also designed and intended to complement and enhance existing systems.

ENERGY INDUSTRY IMPACTS

No matter what the source of fuel that is used to generate today's energy, I see no negative impact to any producer of energy, or utility service provider. If we are to grow this nation and be able to compete internationally in the manufacture of products, then we need all the energy we can produce.

This system would assist our current energy producers in delivering a steady supply of electrical energy to existing factories and population centers and fuel more factories and new population centers in locations where they do not now exist; due to a lack of availability or a consistent supply of energy. We need to keep the cost of production in America low to be competitive with other nations. Also, by having a lower cost for energy, we can have a somewhat higher wage scale and still be competitive. Energy producers that keep their production costs low, while selling and distributing more of it, will make more money.

ANTS will somewhat reduce the need for High Tower Transmission Lines, but not eliminate them. Hopefully, ANTS will be able to provide additional power to locations where these types of transmission systems are not allowed. ANTS will need external power lines and energy stations and regeneration plants along its routes that are connected to the electrical energy cables that it carries inside its structure. It may not contain the highest voltage cables that the High Tower Transmission lines carry, as it will probably have to use smaller size cables instead for safety reasons. It will still use a lot of copper and insulation materials wrapped around all those copper or composite transmission lines.

This system would be part of an overall Energy Strategy that could help our country become Energy Independent. We cannot afford to lose any producer of energy. With respect to our environment, I believe we need to keep on improving those systems that produce energy, yet emit pollutants, and this can be done over time. It does little good for the environment or our country, if you restrict the use of or prohibit a source of fuel here in the United States and not everywhere else in the world. Other countries will obtain the fuel source; they will use it, and those countries might not care as much about the environment as we do.

We can be a world leader in the area of clean energy production by focusing on the technology needed to improve these systems, not by eliminating them.

TRANSPORTATION Industry Impacts

Aviation Industry

The only impact I see to the Aviation industry might be in the competition for intercity and regional transportation. Those flight segments between cities up to 350 miles or so, and only in selected markets as even when ANTS would be fully implemented it still would not have the ability to cover all cities in the United States that Air Transports could serve.

This would tend to impact regional carriers; however, the operators of these businesses might be some of the best operators for the High Speed Ground Transportation operations, and own both an airline and HST line. They already know how to compete with the mega airlines that remain. Also, when someone wants to get to a location fast, they will fly in most cases. But there would be some competition and that is probably a good thing. Furthermore, I believe that international travel to and across the United States will increase when ANTS is implemented, as it provides additional travel options for the international vacation and business traveler.

In regards to manufacturing airplanes, I would think that those companies that build airplanes in America would not be negatively impacted by the new high speed ground transportation systems. On the contrary, I could envision some of the manufacturers of airplanes, automobiles and buses, building equipment for the high speed ground transportation systems. In fact, it was seeing a string of airplane fuselages, being shipped on top of railroad flatbeds that started me thinking about these high speed transport systems, way back when.

Because ANTS will help reduce the unemployment problem there will be more business travelers flying here and there, and consumers will have more disposable income that they can use to take vacations, and travel a lot more.

Automotive Industry

I do not believe the automobile industry will be negatively impacted. The traveling public, whether on business or pleasure will still need transportation in one form or another; for example, car rental or cab, while at their destination. Many people in large urban areas with terrible congestion or parking problems do not own cars or trucks. Besides with the current population not to mention, the projected growth of the population, today's crowded highways often frustrate travelers to the point that they do not want to drive anywhere they do not have to. I believe any reduction in the number of vehicles on the highways, especially, in urban areas would be of benefit in reducing congestion and all the related costs involved with it. Further, if new population centers can be created around the country or existing cities without a current congestion problem grow, they will most likely need and want more ground transportation, in the form of new cars and trucks.

I think the problem automotive manufacturers have today is that too many people cannot afford a new vehicle, due to the lack of JOBS, or good paying jobs. People are holding on to their vehicles for longer periods of time instead of changing models earlier, as they used to do. ANTS, will provide good paying jobs and thus increase the number of people in the middle income level group. If people have more money, they will be able to purchase new vehicles with increasing frequency.

Interstate Highway System

In the foreseeable future, there will always be a need for additional highways and expansion of those existing interstates. However, there are places where ANTS can reduce some congestion on the interstate highway system, and hopefully, the need for adding four more lanes to an eight lane highway in a few places. I believe that would be good in terms of costs and safety. However, I also think that once the ANTS routes are implemented and in use for awhile, there will be more interstate highways needed around new and expanding population centers.

EXISTING FREIGHT RAIL TRANSPORTATION

There would not be any negative impact to the freight train industry. In my opinion, if there is any reduction to the number of conventional passenger rail systems it would be a positive impact as today, freight traffic usually has a lower priority on same use tracks and must be sided (get out of the way) when a passenger train is in the area. This often delays the freight train and delays the delivery of its products it is carrying. Time is money.

EXISTING PASSENGER RAIL TRANSPORTATION

There would be some impact to current passenger rail transportation, over a gradual time period; however, I do not see it replacing existing systems in total. I would also think that any positions lost in existing systems would be migrated to similar positions in ANTS.

HIGH SPEED RAIL AND MAGLEV

I would think that the only impact to those currently involved with High Speed Ground Transportation (HST) in the United States would be positive. It should spur the design and development of HST's by Americans that can eventually compete with the international manufacturers. Hopefully, those involved with designing current routes for high speed ground transportation systems within their state or region would choose to incorporate those plans within ANTS and get involved in the route selection process to ensure their needs are met.

Additional systems will be needed to intersect with the ANTS routes and these can take the shape of several systems in design today. For example, in a state where an ANTS route exists, other high speed ground transports (high speed rail, or MAGLEV) might be needed to cover other areas within that state, and then connect at the ANTS and airport terminals, within that state.

COMMUNICATION Industry Impacts

I cannot think of any potential negative impact to existing communication related systems or providers.

MANUFACTUERING Industry Impacts

There will be some impact to international manufacturers. It is about time. ANTS, along with an energy independent country will provide American manufacturers the tools they need to be competitive with other international free trading countries. We need to keep a high level of manufacturing in the United States. There is plenty of room in the world's markets for competition. Let the best product win.

There are a lot of good people and countries all around the world. Today's Americans just want the opportunity to compete fairly in the domestic and international marketplace; they do not want to eliminate competition. Situations change over time, and there are some products at times that are a better fit for other economic environments than ours, but we do not want to be excluded from any opportunities due to unfair labor, government or environmental practices of any country. We want every countries standard of living to rise. Most Americans realize that we have great trading partners all around the world; especially, our neighbors on both borders of our country. Many of us also realize that free trade is good for democracy, and helps keep the peace!

Project Benefit's

This project can be looked at as a cost savings project. In tandem with work on our country's infrastructure problems, it will over time remove millions of Americans from the unemployment and under employed roles. These working Americans will generate tax revenue for our federal, state and local governments, and help fund programs like Medicare and Social Security.

If we do not resolve long term unemployment, we will continue to spend billions on the necessary survival support for the unemployed. We have and will continue to spend billions on small and short term projects that at best, employ a few people for a short time. Finally, sooner or later, we will unnecessarily spend billions on separate projects like the Energy Grid, interstate highway expansions, and a piecemeal designed high speed ground transportation system that will be inadequate for a country like ours.

THE AMERICAN NATIONAL TRANSPORTATION SYSTEM REDUCES COST

Reduces Unemployment Ranks—General Public, and those Returning volunteers who have served our country or those that are already returned—Service Men & Women

Reduces Food Stamp Expense

Reduces Government Funded Costs for other Critical Support Services

Reduces Foreclosures on Private Housing

Reduces National Debt

Reduces to some extent the:

>Cost of gasoline due to highway congestion

>Cost to install and maintain overhead electrical transmission lines

>Cost to install and maintain long distance communication lines

>Costly delays by freight train haulers due to passenger train traffic on dual purpose rail lines

Cost/Benefit Summary

The American National Transportation System Produces Revenue

Income Tax Revenue for Federal, State, and local Governments from employed workers and companies.

Payroll taxes for funding Social Security (FICA), and Medicare, from employed workers and companies.

State and Local Revenue from Sales Taxes on goods and services from employed workers and businesses.

If enough unemployed become employed, Housing Problem is reduced.

Revenue from fees on sale of power, or leasing of communication lines, and Passenger Ticket Taxes should more than fund maintenance of the system, plus payroll tax revenue from individuals and companies working and operating ANTS.

Unemployed workers and businesses generate no tax revenue.

Additional Benefits—Revenue Streams

Employed Workers with good jobs generally have insurance and money to spend on all types of Medical Care.

Employed Workers generate more sales of Cars and Trucks.

Employed Workers generate more sales of Big Ticket Items.

Employed Workers generate more sales in Consumer Discretionary Items.

Employed Workers spend money on above, and then the recipients of those funds have money to spend, and so on, and so on.

Employed Workers have money to invest, save.

Unemployed workers and businesses spend little on above.

TOURISM INDUSTRY

INDIRECT PROJECT BENEFITS

Tourism is an example of another industry that would benefit from this American National Transportation System project. It would indirectly create more opportunity for the traveling consumer and many new jobs in the industry; travel agencies, cabs, bus and shuttle operators, restaurants, lodgers, tour guides and of course the attractions to which we would go to! We have heard the statement "build it and they will come" and I would modify that slightly to say, "build it and they will use it".

Related statistics for 2010, available from the U.S. Department of Commerce, and its Office of Travel and Tourism Industries, website, **"http://tinet.ita.doc.gov/outreachpages/download_data_table/2010_Key_Facts.pdf"**, show that International travel is the single largest services export from our country and accounts for 25 percent of the total services exported. It states that the United States ranks second overall as an international destination. Who do you think ranks first?

It is interesting to learn that tourism ranks ahead of agricultural goods and motor vehicles in terms of overall exports. Furthermore, the total money spent by travelers to the United States was $134 BILLION DOLLARS, which included $31 billion dollars spent for tickets on U.S. Carriers.

2010 was a record year as we had 60 million visitors to our country! They spent a lot of money too, as we had a trade surplus in this industry of $32 billion dollars, which means that international travelers to the United States spent more in America, than did Americans traveling to international destinations. This is a very interesting website and there are many more statistical facts available, but I feel one of the most important statistics is the fact that the money the international traveler spent here, directly supported 827,000 jobs!

I believe the American National Transportation System (ANTS) project would spur both domestic and international tourism by providing another travel channel that tourists in America do not currently have; High Speed Ground Transportation (HST) whether it be high speed rail or MAGLEV service. The various packages that could be created by professional travel and booking agencies and individuals, would only be limited by their imaginations! Other countries and continents already have these HST services.

The system would be an important piece of and a spark to expanding the United States Tourism industry! It would provide travelers with the capability to tour most of America via all avenues of modern transportation; air service, high speed ground transportation, automotive, driving or riding, visiting and staying wherever they want; all packaged and the cost known up front for the most part. Of course professional services or tourism agencies would create packages with the various carriers, airlines, high speed ground transports, trains, car rentals and lodgers to facilitate a smooth trip. Or the enterprising folks could create their own excursion.

Similar types of packages and trips are already done in other countries and continents and to some extent in the United States. We have some corridors where rail service exists, such as in the Northeast, and that would not go away, nor would those sightseeing rail excursions that cross parts of the continent disappear.

To be competitive for example; If Americans can fly to Paris, see the city and then take the Euro-rail to other locations they wish to visit, why not afford visitors from other countries the same opportunities in the United States. Fly to the states; visit multiple attractions utilizing any mode of transportation they desire.

Well, we are missing a key piece of the transport puzzle today. We do not have convenient, fast ground transportation to marry-up with our excellent air transportation and interstate highway systems. Today, it would be near impossible or challenging for a foreign visitor with a limited time horizon to travel to the United States, and use travel channels other than air transportation or automobile to move about the country, because the missing link does not exist; high speed ground transportation! ANTS!

It can be surprising to find out what foreigners are interested in seeing. Of course, like Americans, they are aware of the normal hot spots, those locations with good weather and famous theme parks, some of our natural wonders, our great cities, and cities that are known for some of the world's greatest gambling and entertainment experiences.

However, there are many who have other interests. For example, there is great interest by some in Jesse James, and seeing where he grew up, as well as Wyatt Earp. Many people have been exposed to these famous or infamous individuals and related locations, Tombstone, Arizona, and Abilene and Dodge City, Kansas, to name a few, through books, novels about the Wild West, and in the last century, with our films.

Recently, I started judging Barbecue Contests as a certified KCS BBQ Judge. At the world famous American Royal Barbecue that is held in Kansas City, Missouri, every fall, I happen to meet some interesting people from another country. The two were from England and they had a keen interest not only in barbecue, but in the old west. One of the pair asked how far away Jesse James had lived from Kansas City; another judge responded that is was just a few miles North from where we were and went on to let him know there were several other related sites close by too. Then the two from England started asking about other outlaws and various locations. I was familiar with some of the names they inquired on, but at the time, that was about it. I was glad others knew the answers to most of their questions. I learned a lot about outlaws and the old west, in a short amount of time. This conversation helped me realize that people around the world, have all sorts of hobbies and interests.

I believe the ANTS project would open up more business for the American Tourism Industry. As I previously related, there are those interested in the Old and Wild West, and some people would like to visit the sites related to Jesse James. But I do not know how many would travel internationally to do only that. However, if after traveling to the mid-west and visiting ST. Joseph and Kearney, Missouri, some of the grounds where Jesse James roamed, they could then catch high speed ground transportation to the Badlands in South Dakota, or the Alamo, in Texas, with perhaps a visit to the Grand Canyon too, before flying home, I believe more people would travel to and explore the United States. That might result in more jobs too.

The good news is that we already have travel agencies, online ticketing facilities, that could put these packages together very easily, including working with airlines, car rental, HST operators, lodging and attractions to create a fun filled vacation limited only by the imagination and one's personal budget.

For example, I have a few suggestions. How about a trip designed to see all the Sports Hall of Fame Attractions for the NFL, NBA, MLB, and Soccer, and maybe some other close by attractions too? To visit these hall of fames you would need to visit; Canton, Ohio for the National Football League, Springfield, Massachusetts for the Naismith Memorial Basketball hall of Fame/National Basketball Association, Cooperstown, New York, for the Major League Baseball Association, and check the website for the Soccer Hall of Fame; it was originally located in Oneonta, New York, but it may have moved. Well, if you are a sports history fan, then the Hall of Fame attractions are not the only game in town. If you are ever in Kansas City, Missouri, for example, check out the Negro Leagues Baseball Museum (NLBM); it is a self guided tour and full of interesting displays and information. Also, while in the city, visit the College Basketball Experience and National Collegiate Basketball Hall of Fame. It too is located in downtown Kansas City, right next to the Sprint Center, where we see a lot of basketball played, and right across the avenue from the Kansas City, Power and Light entertainment venue.

For the history buffs interested in our United States Presidents; what about trips to all the Presidential libraries or since they all do not have presidential libraries, how about where they grew up or lived for some time? Well, then again, since we have several presidents at this point in our history and that might take quite awhile so maybe separate the trips by region like; the West, East, North, South, or Mid West, or even by state. For example, if you visit Virginia, you could visit many related sites; eight presidents were born there and six are buried there.

If you wanted to do a Mid West presidential tour, then you would first select a starting point. Next, figure out your route and plan on using ANTS and rental cars. Maybe start with Harry Truman sites in Independence, Missouri, which is right next to Kansas City, Missouri, and while in the Kansas City area, go to the World War I museum which Harry S. Truman fought in; and then head to Abilene, Kansas for the Eisenhower Library and museum, or south to the Clinton Library in Little Rock, Arkansas—maybe this one would be considered a southern tour. If true, then instead off to West Branch, Iowa for the Herbert Hoover Library. After that, head to Springfield, Illinois for a visit to the Abraham Lincoln, museum; other options might include the Ronald Regan Museum in Eureka, Illinois, and the Ulysses S. Grant home in Galena, Illinois.

If you get tired of history why not change the theme to food! I am a BBQ fanatic and hope you are too. My recommendation would be to start your BBQ trip in Kansas City, Missouri, and the general metropolitan area which even includes some areas in Kansas. Some of us call it the BBQ capital of the world. I would time my trip to include the American Royal BBQ Competition which starts in late September, and plan to spend a few days sampling BBQ from around the world at the competition; and around the KC area, sampling some of the wonderful BBQ diners available in metropolitan area and yes there are too many to name them here.

Still hungry for BBQ! Then onto the airport in Memphis, Tennessee for some of their BBQ; they used to have a couple of places right in the terminal area. Ok, they have some great BBQ all over that city too. While in the area include a stop at Graceland, then head to Texas to sample their BBQ. Come to think of it, while in Texas, why not visit the Alamo and San Antonio.

My last example of using the imagination to plan a trip using all modes of transportation, including ANTS is: how about a tour of the Music Hall of fame attractions? Start off the trip by visiting the Rock and Roll hall of fame in Cleveland, Ohio. Then head to Detroit, Michigan to visit the Motown Museum. After that, then off to Nashville's country music hall of fame, saving a couple of days for a visit to Branson, Missouri; the capital of entertainment in the mid-west some say, and then back home via the mode of transportation you choose.

America is a beautiful country with many natural and created attractions waiting to be visited. I believe the ANTS project will have a very positive impact on the Tourism industry in the United States, from both a domestic and international viewpoint. It will begin as soon as the first leg of the system is in place. The American National Transportation System complements the other modes of transportation involved with tourism by providing high speed ground transportation; a new travel option within our county. That is good for the traveling consumer and business!

Just remembered that previously, I had mentioned that in 2010, the United States ranked second as the most popular destination for international travelers, but forgot to mention who was first. It was France.

CHAPTER 5

How to Finance the Project

That old saying, "It takes money to make money" is true! I believe the American National Transportation System (ANTS) has the potential overtime to directly and indirectly create a couple million jobs. These employees' will make money and have money to spend. Investors, businesses and material suppliers of all sorts will also have the opportunity to make money and have money to spend and even reinvest in other projects. However, like most things that are worth doing, it will take some work, and some money to get this project started, funded and operational.

Call me an optimist, but even in today's world, I believe a majority of Americans would support important projects like we used to do, if we had confidence that we could TRUST whoever was in charge of the project. The interstate highway system, the space program, and even the cold war, to name a few, are examples of projects in the past that a majority of the American people supported.

For many Americans, we just need to know the basics. We want to understand what the project is about; especially, the needs and benefits for the project. We accept that either up front, or in the end we will pay for it. Still, at the beginning we need to know how it is to be paid for or funded, and who is in charge or responsible for the project. We need a sense that someone or group can be trusted, and is responsible for keeping track of and using the money expended in a proper manner.

We hate hearing stories about someone spending $100 dollars of our tax money, for a $10 dollar hammer! We want someone held responsible for these excesses and waste of our tax dollars; that is why we want to know who is in charge of the project. Americans are a forgiving people and understand that mistakes do happen, but when the public senses corruption, it loses trust and it can take a long time to regain it.

In these matters, some say that the American people have short memories or that we just lose interest quicker than most. But I believe many Americans do not have the time nor desire to follow projects or events, on anything but a periodic basis. Many of us feel that we have elected our representatives to do this job, and we trust them to do it. We also depend on the press to keep an eye on them.

Funding Methods

Methods to fund the ANTS and the Infrastructure work.

In America today, there are new funding and operating practices being used all over our country, in addition to those traditional sources we are most familiar with to fund and operate projects. I have outlined three methods for funding the American National Transportation System below. I realize that there are probably more ways for it to be funded and controlled, and would be interested in getting educated on any other methods or suggestions you might have.

Funding the ANTS Project—Traditional Method

If the traditional method is used to fund this project then the process will work in this manner. Congress appropriates the funds; then whatever cabinet department or independent commission that will be responsible for the ANTS project, would utilize those funds to get the project moving with funding for a period of time. Then as that time period expires, the process of reauthorization of funds would then occur on a scheduled basis, such as from year to year.

This method could follow a similar path as does the interstate highway system. The states would also have similar funding responsibilities as they do currently, with costs for their portion of the interstate highway system. As most are aware, we the people paid for construction of the national interstate highway system; and are still paying for maintaining it today, along with any new construction.

Every gallon of gas that you purchase has a federal tax and also a state tax that goes into the fund that pays for the interstate highway system. In some places they even have a local tax added to it. In some states they also use toll roads to collect fees to fund their highways and infrastructure expenses.

The American National Transportation System (ANTS) could be funded by taxing high speed ground transportation (HST) passenger tickets, in the same way an airline passenger ticket is taxed. Additionally, the fees from the ANTS energy and communication components would be applied to the fund too. In theory, this money would be directed toward an account to fund ANTS.

The traditional method would work for funding the ANTS project. However, one of its drawbacks is that it might lengthen the startup and delivery time of the project, and thus many of the benefits. Additionally, it could easily become a *political football game*, every time the funding needed to be reauthorized.

FUNDING THE ANTS PROJECT—SELL BONDS

The next method for funding the American National Transportation System (ANTS), along with a fund for repairing our countries existing infrastructure would be through a specific bond issue at the national level. To some, this might seem a little far-fetched; but I say why not? State and local governments issue bonds from time to time, for funding specific projects; why not the federal government?

The United States Treasury Department already sells treasury notes, bonds, and of course the U.S. Savings bonds. All these bonds can be purchased by the consumer. I am also aware that other funding sources are occasionally made available, that provide government agencies, states, and even local governments access to specific government bonds; an example would be the $25 billion dollars of Recovery Zone bonds that were issued in 2009. These were designed for states and local governments to use for economic recovery purposes. However, as far as I know, there are not currently any bonds for specific purposes that the consumer can buy.

I did some research on the internet and found out that the federal government has sold specific bonds to consumers before; they were called war bonds. Although I was not around when the government last sold war bonds, during World War II, I did remember seeing them referenced in many of the older movies and documentaries. They used the stars of that era to promote them and help create a sense that all Americans have a stake in the war effort. These bonds had actually existed prior to the start of the war, and were called Defense Bonds. An interesting fact about these war bonds is that purchasers of these bonds made a rate of return that was less than what they could get at a local bank. There was a great sense of patriotism back then, and I do not believe the ANTS bonds could be sold below market value, in today's economy.

I am not sure how the process would work to have specific U.S. Bonds issued for the ANTS and Infrastructure projects, but I am pretty sure that this would be a legitimate method to raise funds for these two projects.

Since, at this time in our history, rates to borrow money are so low, I have some ideas that might make these new bonds unique and attractive to the American consumer. It might help create a sense of ownership in these projects too.

In general, these government issued bonds would be tax free in the same manner as are other U.S. Treasury bonds and notes, with a decent payout rate. Following are potential guidelines for the ANTS and Infrastructure U.S. Bonds.

- They could only be sold to U.S. Citizens
- Social security number required to purchase
- Upper limit on the amount individual could buy/own would be 50K or 100K.
- U.S Government backed guarantee
- Possibly one quarter or one half point above the going treasury rate for a ten year note; interest would/could be paid semi annually with a length of 5 or 10 years to maturity, or sold discounted and face value paid at maturity.
- Inflation Protected Possibly

The proceeds from the sale of these bonds would be split evenly and deposited into separate accounts; one used only for financing the American National Transportation System, and the other account used only for funding the catastrophic infrastructure projects. The proceeds from these bonds, minus expenses to sale them and pay interest on them if applicable, and at redemption, would be deposited into national and state banks within the several states rather than one large national account.

Congress and administrative departments working with the states, would be responsible for determining what infrastructure projects would be addressed and in what priority. To ensure the funding for infrastructure repairs is fairly distributed among all the states, they would take into consideration; the severity of the problem and number of projects already active or funded within each state.

I believe that a majority of citizens would be all for a funding method of this nature, if they could be confident that the money raised would be used for the express purpose that the bonds were issued for and not be siphoned off to other areas of government. Today, Americans have a lack of confidence and trust in our government and some of our private business concerns. A successful completion of a project like the American National Transportation System using government issued specific bonds to fund the project, would go a long way to restoring confidence and trust in the American Government.

Selling specific bonds to fund the American National Transportation System (ANTS) and our nation's major infrastructure problems would be a viable method for raising the money. I think a beneficial difference from the traditional method is that all the money would be allocated and in an account; ready to use. You would not have to reauthorize funds for the project on a periodic basis, and it would be left out of the political process, hopefully. The bonds would be paid off in the same manner as in the traditional method.

Funding ANTS—Public Private Partnerships (P 3's)

A third alternative method for funding the American National Transportation System (ANTS) is probably considered more modern in its nature than the previously discussed methods. Today in the United States, there are other means to finance efforts like the infrastructure repair projects, and expansion of electric energy transmission systems. CNBC provided an insight to these sources when it aired its special on infrastructure problems called, "The Race to Rebuild America's Infrastructure" back in November of 2011. I thought it was an eye opener into the depth of problems we face in America regarding problems with our aging roads, bridges and other infrastructure systems.

The program discussed "P 3's" which are Government and Business partnerships (Public, Private, Partnerships) and provided a little information on how these work. I did some additional research on these arrangements and discovered they are occurring all around the country. It seems the primary reason they are so popular now is that other methods for totally financing large government projects are not readily available. Some of these projects could get partial financing through the traditional funding methods which may get the project started, but the project may not get completed because as time goes on and additional funding is needed, it cannot be obtained. This might be the reason you may have read or heard about a road or other government project that was started, but never completed; it is probably waiting on funding.

The other side of these financial arrangements (P 3's) requires the government to turn over some level of operating rights or control to the P3 Company. This contract is usually for a long time period; perhaps somewhere in the 25 to 75 year range. It usually allows the P3 business to set fees at a level that will produce the desired return on their investment.

This CNBC show featured an interesting project that began in Indiana, 2006. The State of Indiana contracted with two foreign companies; CINTRA from Spain and MACQUARIE from Australia, through an investor group called RTR Concession Company that runs the project. The project is a 157 mile toll road and the state signed a 75 year lease with the RTR Company to rebuild, operate and maintain it. Additionally, the State of Indiana received $4 billion dollars at the signing to use on other projects around the state.

Note: the RTR Concession Company has increased the toll from around $4.00 in 2006 to $9.00 in 2011. Opposition from groups like U.S. PIRG (a federation of Public Interest Research Groups); see website http://www.uspirg.org/about, for more information on this subject, do not like these arrangements and equates this to providing a monopoly. The Chief Operations Officer for the RTR Concession Company disagrees and says people are not forced to use the toll road but do so, because it is safe, fast and well maintained, all paid for by the operating company, and ultimately by the user of the road.

So, an additional means of funding the American National Transportation System (ANTS) could be through partnerships between the state and federal governments, and private business concerns. Since ANTS is a large national project, it might work best using a combination of funding methods spread across and covering different parts of the system. The federal and state governments would have regulatory responsibility over the energy, communications and passenger transportation components, and perhaps some authority to control excessive fees to the end user of the energy and communications components.

I can envision that several different Joint Venture companies would be formed to; construct and maintain the basic system of the ANTS platform, and then companies to operate and maintain the facilities related to the different components; Energy, Communications, and High Speed Transportation. Each of the three ANTS components requires different technical expertise and existing companies would risk less if they joined with other companies in their field of expertise to handle that component.

Examples have been mentioned previously (see chapter 3, energy component) as in the joint effort in Indiana, to build additional high voltage power lines, by the Duke and American Electric Power companies. The same type of expertise and risk sharing might be found useful by the communication network companies. The one component that might require a little more government oversight might be in the high speed transportation component.

I envision that there will be public and private operators using the passenger transportation component of the system, just as occurs today in the airline industry. Airlines operate under the regulation and control of the Federal Aviation Administration (FAA), and I would also believe that a similar group such as the Federal Railway Administration (FRA) would be needed to set guidelines and regulations for safety and speed, and monitor High Speed Ground Transportation (HST) operators to ensure compliance. However, I could see a private business concern doing a similar activity for the High Speed Ground Transportation (HST) system (monitoring and controlling traffic) as does the aircraft controllers do for the airline operators. Another model for this system of scheduling, controlling and monitoring movement might be found in today's surface railroad system, where multiple railroad companies for both freight and passenger services exist and sometimes share the same tracks.

SUMMARY OF FUNDING METHODS

The traditional method of appropriating funds using the general treasury account, and the method of selling bonds to raise the money adds to the National Debt. Although, over time the funds borrowed would be repaid by the ANTS project itself, through income taxes on those now employed, and through fee collections associated with the three components (energy, communications and passenger transportation) operating within the system, once it is implemented.

The government has to be involved in this project at some level, but in these first two methods, they would be heavily involved from the start to the finish. Without regard to any political parties, many people would have some concerns that the normal course of politics would delay the project and its benefits. Some might even argue that our government already has its hands full with other matters.

Using Public, Private, Partnerships (P3's) to fund this project would not add to the National Debt. As with the other two methods, government treasuries would be the recipient of tax revenue from all the new workers and businesses involved with building and operating the American National Transportation System. However, in return for funding the project, the private business partner(s) would want the authority and control to manage the project as they would in any private contract, and then establish prices that would provide a return on their investments. The project would most likely progress faster and the primary purpose of the ANTS project is to create good jobs.

Above all, I believe the American National Transportation System needs to be done. It is important to remember that it has the potential to reinvigorate our countries manufacturing industries. There are too many people unemployed and underemployed not to do it. We are already paying billions of dollars for this high level of unemployment in the form of unemployment compensation, economic support via food stamps and other necessary support systems. It also negatively contributes to the housing problem.

If I had to make the decision on which funding method to use, I believe I would choose a combination of public and private financing. State and federal governments have to be involved initially, and ongoing, as well. The government (that would be us) would provide some initial funds to get the project designed and then contract with private concerns to manufacture, construct, and operate the system.

CHAPTER 6

CONGRESSIONAL ACTION

The American National Transportation System is a large project and will need much support and effort to make it a reality. We will need leaders in government and the private sector who can work together to make this a successful endeavor.

In the following sections, I have outlined what I believe are some of the milestones necessary for this project to get started and moved along through the processes involved in a project like the American National Transportation System. In particular, I have provided a high level description of the Congressional processes that an IDEA goes through before becoming legislation.

Finally, I have provided an operational model for this project that hopefully highlights many of the steps involved in the decision making process and key roles for control, operations and auditing functions for this project. I chose a combination of public and private financing to use in the model as I believe it best fits the financial needs of this project. It also gives all sectors a stake in the project. Furthermore, we now have the experience in using the Public, Private, Partnerships (P3's) for getting projects financed and completed. We can draw on this expertise to create the proper and responsible legislation, contracts, and operating plans to make this project a successful reality.

ESTABLISH THE ANTS PROJECT—DETERMINE RESPONSIBILITY

The congressional experts and the executive administration would know where the responsibility fits best. Should it be created under one of the Departments associated with the project, such as the Department of Transportation, Department of Energy, Department of the Interior, or some other department. Should it be a separate commission or an organization like NASA? For example, the interstate highway system and related projects come under the responsibility of the federal and state's departments of transportation. Anything to do with energy generation and management are a responsibility of the department of energy. And all communication networks, cables and transmissions are under the responsibility of the Federal Communications Commission (FCC).

I do not know if the ANTS project is large enough to be setup as a new NASA type organization or a permanent commission like the Federal Communications Commission. Besides, we already have a number of cabinet level departments that could handle this project.

Once responsibility and ownership are determined a bill or legislation must be created so that the legislative process can begin.

BACKGROUND ON THE CONGRESSIONAL PROCESS

Congress has two main parts, bodies, or chambers to it; the House of Representatives and the Senate. Within each part, it divides up the legislative categories or responsibilities into groups or committees, as members in either chamber cannot be experts on every issue. Each committee has a chairperson that heads up that committee too. For example, there are groups within each body that focus on agricultural issues, energy, defense, transportation, and several other categories.

Apparently, there are two committees for each group as well. For example, in the House of Representatives you would have a committee for agriculture authorizations, and another committee for agriculture appropriations. Members that serve on the authorization committee for agriculture introduce bills and review related legislation and decide if the legislation moves forward or not for the general consideration of Congress. Members that serve on the appropriations committee for agriculture would review these bills or legislation and decide if they will be funded or not. If the appropriation committee approves the bill or legislation, then eventually Congress gives the Treasury department the OK to write the check.

Note: Members from the agriculture authorization committee do not serve on the agriculture appropriation committee or vice versa. It works the same for all categories or areas of legislation.

This makes sense to me as you would not want representatives to have control over both the project introduction and submission process and the project review and approval funding process. It is a good check and balance and audit control process.

UNDERSTANDING THE CONGRESSIONAL PROCESS

Although I watch a lot of television, I have not seen any programs having to do with this process so I did some studying to educate myself on the legislative process. I reviewed our constitution and some other reference books on the subject, at the library. The constitution does not take that long to read, but for me, comprehending it, was another matter.

Later, I did some searches on the internet and found many articles and information on the legislative process that I feel provides at least a high level understanding of what is involved with getting a project like the American National Transportation System started and moved through the process.

Here are a few websites that I reviewed that provide in my mind a good but digested outline of the process. First, I recommend you review an article on About.com, written by Robert Longley, website, http://usgovinfo.about.com/od/uscongress/a/legprocess.htm. It is called How Bills Become Laws or Not, and it provides a 14 step guide about how laws are introduced and processed from their origination all the way through Congress and if necessary, action taken by Congress if it has been vetoed by the president. Next, I recommend you review an article called, "Authorization and Appropriation", by GalleryWatch.com, at the website, http://www.llrx.com/congress/authorization.htm. This will give you a synopsis of the process involved in getting the legislation moving on the ANTS project. This article by Paul Jenks was published on January 15, 2007, but I am sure it still applies today.

Another short summary of the process worth reviewing on the internet is provided by Gale encyclopedia of US History; an article called, "Appropriations by Congress", website: http://www.answers.com/topic/appropriations-by-congress. It describes aspects of the process and also has several links to relevant definitions.

Congress would have a key role in getting the American National Transportation System project started and moving through the conception phase to the development phase in a timely fashion. As described in some of the previous descriptions, the ANTS project could be held up, stalled or even tabled at many points in the process. Since the primary funding for this project will come from the private sector and with the benefits to the country in the area of job creation, and income for the United States Treasury, I am counting on bipartisan support from our Congress. Additionally, this is an opportunity for our Congressional representatives to prove to the country that they can work together to accomplish something important and beneficial for America.

I hope from this brief description of the legislative process you can understand why it is so important to let your congressional representative and your senator's know your desires with respect to supporting this addition to the American National Transportation System and the millions of jobs that will be created by this project!

STARTING THE PROCESS

ESTABLISH THE ANTS PROJECT—AUTHORIZATION PHASE

The first step in the process is to get a bill introduced in the House of Representatives and the Senate, to create and authorize the American National Transportation System (ANTS) project. I am assuming that in this case it would be handled by congressional representation on the Transportation and Infrastructure committee of each body. However, I could be incorrect, since ANTS is significantly involved in the electrical energy and communications areas, in addition to High Speed Ground Transportation (HST).

ESTABLISH THE ANTS PROJECT—APPROPRIATION PHASE

The second step in the process is to get the authorized bill approved for funding, in both the House of Representatives, and the Senate.

Sometimes there are differences between versions of the similar legislation and when there are, they have to be reconciled.

FUNDING METHOD
SELECTED—COMBINATION PUBLIC/PRIVATE

Using a combination of public and private financing to fund the project, would require congress to appropriate the "seed" money for the initial project study, the high level project scope and route selections. In relative terms this should not be a huge expense, and if necessary, they could possibly obtain the funds from the various department budgets that are involved; Transportation, Interior, Energy, Commerce, Environmental Protection Agency, and some from the defense budget as this project supports aspects of our country's national security.

While this phase of the project is underway, private businesses would work with the government team (P3 relationships) in a collaborative environment. Businesses would be able to bid for the work by route, and take over the subsequent phases of the project, including financing the project.

Having been a project manager on many projects during my career in Information Technology, I learned through experience that having the organization and responsibilities clearly identified at the outset makes for a smoother process and provides the means for a successful completion.

I know that we have excellent people in the private and public sectors that are more qualified and skilled in creating an organizational plan for a project like this American National Transportation System (ANTS), than I am. However, after thinking about all the different public and private groups that would be involved with this project, I became intrigued with the idea of setting up a basic organization and plan that could possibly handle the task. Therefore, I have provided some thoughts on organization and responsibilities and described these efforts using the team concept.

Organization Model

Organizational Plan for the ANTS Project

Overall, there would be three teams. Team One would have the task of getting the project scoped out, including the initial five routes, refining, and detail designing of the platform and components requirements and estimates. Team two would be involved with selecting the management of the project, and team three would have an auditing and oversight role.

Organization:

Team one would be formed using existing personnel from the departments of Transportation, Interior, Energy, Environmental Protection Agency and Federal Communications Commission for the purpose of creating the American National Transportation System (ANTS) project. They would be responsible for planning and detailing the initial five routes; drafting regulations and codes for the construction of the platform, including guidelines and specifications on all the components. They would utilize existing interstate high way route plans wherever possible, right of ways, and work with state planning commissions with respect to each of the five initial routes. Additionally, they would ensure that the slots for the High Speed Ground Transportation equipment accommodate as applicable, international sizes and standards for high speed rail, and MAGLEV operations.

Team one would also work with component related private engineering and design firms in designing and drafting all the regulations and codes that will apply to designing, manufacturing, and construction of the ANTS platform, and all related components. There work will be subject to approval by the relevant congressional committee for the component area; for example, any energy related issue could be reviewed and addressed by the congressional committee on energy. Any issue a state might have could also be addressed through the congressional review process in addition to discussion with the department involved in the issue.

TEAM ONE

CONGRESS works with Cabinet Departments – They will supply expert staff and work with Public, State, and Private concerns including technical experts from communication, energy, and transportation concerns to create project plans, designs & high level estimates.

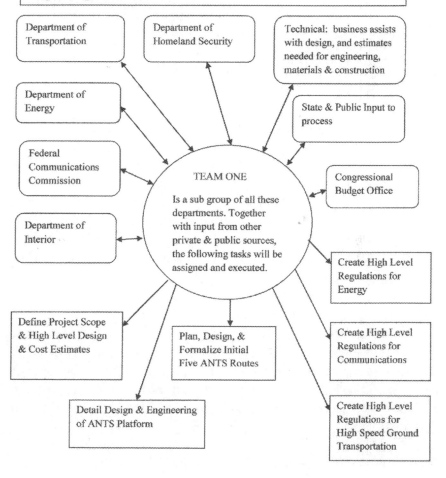

Department of Transportation

Department of Homeland Security

Technical: business assists with design, and estimates needed for engineering, materials & construction

Department of Energy

State & Public Input to process

Federal Communications Commission

TEAM ONE

Is a sub group of all these departments. Together with input from other private & public sources, the following tasks will be assigned and executed.

Congressional Budget Office

Department of Interior

Create High Level Regulations for Energy

Define Project Scope & High Level Design & Cost Estimates

Plan, Design, & Formalize Initial Five ANTS Routes

Create High Level Regulations for Communications

Detail Design & Engineering of ANTS Platform

Create High Level Regulations for High Speed Ground Transportation

Another team (team two) would be created and they would select the management of the American National Transportation System (ANTS) project for the first five routes. I do not have any idea on what the composition of this team would be; I suppose that the administration in consultation with congress would nominate this person as I believe is done today with other similar positions.

This team would select the commissioner and this person would be in overall charge of the project. The commissioner would then select five directors; one for each of the initial routes and each director would be primarily responsible for everything to do with their route. They would report directly to the commissioner. All would be subject to congressional approval.

This team would work with the states involved in each route; select and contract with P3 type businesses or organizations that would manufacture, construct, and install the ANTS platform within each of their routes, along with materials for the energy and communication components. This team would be responsible for all budgeting and other fiduciary matters, including reporting to congress and other parties. Also, they would be responsible for ensuring payment to the treasury and the dedicated ANTS fund, of any funds due from P3 organizations contracted.

Another team (Team three) would be formed that would review all regulations and standards created by the first team and working with professional engineering firms ensure they make sense and that any unnecessary regulations or constraints are corrected. Members of this team would also inspect manufacturing facilities, materials, construction and assembly aspects of the platforms and components as they are developed.

Members of this team would be from the private and public sector. They would include experts in design, engineering, manufacturing and construction for the components of the system. Their main purpose would be to ensure that all codes were met with the use of proper materials and a solid product is developed from the beginning through the end of the project. An example of participates in this team might be; the civil engineers of America.

Another responsibility of this team would be to review all large contracts that the second team makes regarding contracts with P3's, to ensure they are fair and that competitive bidding was properly used as might be requested by congress. This should help spread the wealth between many design, manufacturing and materials companies of all sizes. This team would consult with state legislatures who would then work with congressional representatives to resolve any major issues. If necessary, this team would also consult with U.S. Congressional committees.

I am all for using American built equipment and note that some sentiments and legislation may exist for applying this philosophy to the new high speed transportation in America. However, we preach "Free Market Enterprise" as we like to market our products, including Aerospace equipment around the world. We are upset when companies like Boeing are not treated fairly when trying to compete with other international businesses; some that are country sponsored or owned businesses, in industry related sales. Therefore, with respect to High Speed Ground Transportation (HST) equipment, I believe we should strive to use domestic equipment makers whenever it is feasible, but not mandate it. Any issues arising in this area should be reviewed and resolved by team two.

We should expect and acknowledge that there are several foreign countries and nations' way ahead of us in the area of High Speed Ground Transportation (HST), which would include High Speed Rail and MAGLEV operators. There are already American Companies partnering with foreign high speed ground transportation companies and they all should be able to operate their equipment on ANTS so long as our standards are met.

Any rail line carrier operator could use any manufacturer's equipment on these tracks. Just like airlines do today; they often have equipment (aircraft) from more than one manufacturer, for example, Airbus, and Boeing. There is also space for MAGLEV operators and the philosophy would be the same with respect to those equipment makers.

The domestic high speed ground transportation carrier operators would be majority owned by Americans, following the same ownership parameters as do the domestic airline carrier operators.

Eventually, this would provide the ultimate means for comparison and competition and open the door for American businesses to compete internationally in the field of high speed ground transportation equipment manufacturers. Once we gain experience and apply innovation and ingenuity to these systems, we would be able to demand the right to compete with other countries in exporting our equipment to foreign operators of High Speed Ground Transportation systems.

Therefore, for the high speed ground transportation portion of the American National Transportation System, I would encourage Domestic Operators, to use U.S. manufactured equipment whenever possible, but also permit them to use equipment and operational software designed or constructed outside of the United States for their high speed passenger transportation operations.

CHAPTER 7

How to Support the Project

Lobby!

We all hear about the bad lobbyists that have so much influence over our government representatives. What can be done about this? Well, as the old saying goes; "if you can't beat them, join them". Might as well become one; but be a good lobbyist! It is a fundamental right we have and some might even say it is our duty. Really, it seems unfair to complain too much about what your representative voted for or against, if we do not let them know once in awhile, what we would like them to support?

Many representatives will send out questionnaires seeking your feedback and input on issues of the day. Yes, it may be true that professional lobbyists have more resources and influence than individuals do, but I still think that if our representatives know what their constituents want or what issues concern them, they will have cause to pay attention. So, send e-mails and call congressional representatives and senator's at both the FEDERAL and STATE levels. Ask them what the status of the ANTS project is? Tell them you want to be kept informed and would they please put you on their contact list; many routinely send e-mails or mail correspondence out to their constituents. They even have conference meetings over the telephone that you can participate in.

It is fairly easy to find out who your congressional representatives are if you do not already know. We each have just one representative in the House of Representatives that comes from the congressional district we vote in! We each have two senators for the state that we vote in! You can always mail them a note. You can even call their office in Washington, DC, or their local offices if you prefer. If you have access to the internet and need help locating your representatives, use the websites listed in the appendices under the section, References and Selected Internet Sites.

You might ask a friend or relative for help; or maybe even go to the library and they can often assist you. Again, ask your government representatives to support the American National Transportation System (ANTS) project and request that they please keep you informed on the status of the ANTS project.

News Organizations: Contact news organizations via face book, twitter, e-mail, phone or regular mail and ask them if they know what the status is of the ANTS project?

Elections: 2012 is an election year. Ask those seeking your vote, whether they are in office or running for the position, what their position is on the ANTS project. Your vote counts! In many congressional districts and senate races winning or losing his or her election is often a matter of a few thousand votes or even less. You only need to be concerned about your own representatives. Let them know that you support ANTS and want them to support it too. Ask them to take action and help get this project moving. Also, if they are in office, ask them to keep you informed of this project's progress.

Check with other people or relatives you know and urge them to do the same. Even if these folks do not normally vote it would help if they contacted their representative too! For example, one of my brothers watches more television than I; follows and stays up on all the issues, yet he seldom votes. I will work with him and urge him to contact his representatives. I will even get his representatives contact information for him. Remember, be a lobbyist; it will only take a few minutes of your time. Our representatives want and need your input.

AARP: Do you belong to this organization? I Do. E-mail or write them and tell them you want to support this project and could they follow up on the status of the project in the monthly magazine. You can contact AARP Member services by telephone at: 1-888-687-2277 or send an E-mail to: member@aarp.org, or write to the Editorial Office at address: 601 E. St NW, Washington, DC 20049.

Veterans: Whether you belong to a related organization or not, I would urge you to support the ANTS project. If you are a member of a veteran's organization, urge your local organizations support for this project and let your representatives know about it! Americans appreciate your service no matter when it occurred or whether it was voluntary or not. I am confident that this project will create many opportunities for veterans who are seeking a good job. I am especially hopeful that this project will have positions and opportunities, for those who are known today, as wounded warriors, and for those families whose warrior did not come home.

Project Contacts: Keep up with the project status via the ANTS Project website: http://ants-status.com/, or through e-mail (ants. status@gmail.com).

CHAPTER 8

Unemployment

The following are some of my thoughts, observations, and opinions on the causes of unemployment and underemployment, along with some related statistics I have gathered through my research for the American National Transportation System.

Since the late spring of 2011, I have been noticing something about workers at the various stores, malls, and fast food restaurants. There are many middle aged and older folks working at some of these jobs; the type of jobs that I used to do when I was a teenager. I am not referring to the senior citizens who may be supplementing their retirement or social security income.

After casual conversations with some of these workers, I learned that several of them had more than one job; this is what I refer to as underemployed. They need more than one job to pay the bills, rent or mortgage, medical expenses and put food on the table. Besides the pay issue it seems that in many cases employers are reluctant to hire full time workers. Most of these folks seemed liked good people, good workers, and I believe they have not given up trying to make a better living for themselves and their families. I hope our economy can provide more opportunities for them very soon.

Teenage Unemployment

Another problem highlighted by statistics relative to unemployment is the teenager and young adult unemployment rate. During the summer of 2011, some cities reported that they had teenager unemployment at over 50 percent. Some of these statistics are based on surveys of teenagers looking for a job, but are unable to find one. You can check the numbers out for yourself by searching "unemployment rate for teenagers" as there are many sites with data and analysis related to this subject. For example, the bureau of labor statistics does a periodic household survey and the data that was made available on the December, 2, 2011, reference website http://www.bls.gov/news.release/empsit.nr0.htm, shows that overall the teenage unemployment rate was at 23.7 percent, for November, 2011.

There are lots of articles available, and much analysis has been done on this subject of teenager unemployment. Following are some of the more common and agreed upon reasons for such high unemployment in this age group.

One cause often suggested is the lack of available funding for teenage employment during the summer due to budget constraints on cities all over the country. Others, blame the high minimum wage, while others say that it is the use of automation that has eliminated some previously held youth jobs. The general softness of the economy and lack of consumer spending is also mentioned as a cause of teenage unemployment. Finally, some even point to many older people now holding some of these jobs as another part of the problem.

I remember when I was a teenager, it seemed you could with a little effort, get part time work during the summer, and job availability during the school year was even better. You may have heard people say that today's young people just do not want to work, but in regard to that sentiment, I do not believe that it is any different today than when I was a kid, in that, some kids that do not have to work, probably are not going to go out of their way to find a job. However, for those young people who need a job the pickings are slim, just as they are for many adults. As previously mentioned, one of the realities of today's economy and job market is that many adults are trying to make a living and are holding some of the jobs that the young folks traditionally held in an earlier time in America.

POVERTY LEVELS AND THE MINIMUM WAGE

Other discussions that I have listened to centered on why there are so few good paying jobs available. First of all there might be some argument as to what is a good paying job. Some would argue that any job is a good job and there is probably truth to that statement. I would agree that in addition to being paid for your labor, there are intangible benefits to holding a job too, such as self worth, and respect.

The health and human resources department have guidelines concerning the determination for the level of poverty in our country; in other words, are you in or out of poverty. For example, from my reading of the charts, a household of four requires income above $22,350 to be above the poverty line. The information on their website does not state whether it is a family of four, just the number of persons in the household, and this covers all states except, Alaska and Hawaii.

I think that depending on where you reside, that may or may not cut it. Either way, that is not a lot of income if spread amongst four people; especially, when you consider the prices of goods and services today. The federal minimum wage is $7.25 per hour and at 40 hours per week that comes to $15,080 per year by my calculations. Even if you double that to $30,160 it might be hard for a family of four to make it in some places, and of course that also depends on whether you have any other benefits with your job; mainly health insurance coverage.

REASONS FOR HIGH UNEMPLOYMENT LEVELS

Some say the high unemployment level is due to using technology to make companies more productive and thus they need fewer employees. Others, blame "right sizing" that occurs as a result of companies merging or acquiring one another to form a larger company and thus consolidating many jobs. Still others, say the main culprit is shipping jobs out of the country, to cheaper labor markets or where governments do not have much regard for pollution control. All these reasons and others are probably all true to an extent. I spent some time thinking about these issues, with respect to contributing to the unemployment problem in America today, and briefly discuss a few of these issues in the following.

There is little doubt that technological innovations and improvements have eliminated and or modified many jobs. Having been in the information technology field for many years, I have seen it replace many manual tasks and eliminate some jobs. I know that it has done the same in a lot of industries and to a lot of jobs, including assembly line work. On the other hand, it is also true that many jobs have been created because of technological innovations, and in some instances, some very good jobs. A formula may exists that shows the number of jobs lost due to technology versus jobs gained in technology, but I have never seen it and would be skeptical of the resulting numbers; too many variables. However, excluding implements of warfare, I think it can be argued that most of the improvements and advances in science and technology have made it a better and safer world in which to work and live. Besides, I have no idea how you could limit the use of technology to save jobs, even if you wanted to in a free society.

With regards to companies merging or one taking over another, many of us have witnessed, or experienced it ourselves, the resulting impact that often occurs when one company buys or merges with another company. Does it seem to you that sooner or later in these situations, employees of the company that was taken over no longer have jobs?

This can occur whether it is a friendly merger or a hostile takeover situation. In these mergers and acquisitions, one message you can just about count on hearing is a related public announcement from those involved, that states, "this event will have little or no affect on the jobs of local employees". Personally, I have never had a major problem with one company, public or private, paying cash or some stock swap for another, as I have always understood that is just the way it is suppose to work in a free market economy. However, I have always wondered if it is a good idea to be able to obtain another company, especially a competitor, by borrowing the money from a lender and basing the loan on the assets of the company being acquired. Then after acquiring the target company, selling off those assets to pay back the loan. There is something wrong with that type of transaction, in my opinion.

How about the major airlines for one example; where once there were many, now there are few. Some say deregulation of the airline industry is to blame. Others, say it was the cost of labor and later the cost of fuel that has eliminated so many of our major airlines. No matter the reason, from what I have observed, it seems that in most cases where competing companies are merged you are bound to lose some jobs; and from a consumer point of view, it also removes some competition from the marketplace. Bottom line, it adds people to the unemployment rolls.

One thought that my late father in law, Charles E. Gregory, said over 35 years ago when his company shut down, was that this country is going to a bad place (I modified his actual statement). He was a Korean War era veteran who had started working in the garment manufacturing industry even before leaving to serve our country, and upon completing his service, returned to his job. His company closed down in the 1970's. What he used to do was now being done in one of those countries with cheaper labor. For awhile, he found employment at smaller shops that tried to compete against those foreign labor based companies, but eventually, they went out of business too. I also remember that at family gatherings, whenever he received a birthday or Christmas present, he would always look at the label to see where it was made; clothes, tools, any product, and would shout loudly whenever he received a present that was not made in the USA. After awhile, he quit shouting about it but I still saw him looking at those labels. I think about this just about every time I see an advertisement on television about buying some product that is made in America, as they lament how it keeps someone in America in a job.

Around the time the manufacturing jobs began leaving the United States, or as some call it outsourcing, really got moving, the technological or information technology boom was also off and running. Many employment experts of the day said that it is the nature of things, and that all those who used to work in manufacturing had to do, was get trained in the new technology jobs; become a computer operator or programmer, or perhaps, start your own business. Many tried, and some succeeded, but on the whole, not everyone is cut out to build robots, design and create software or operate their own business.

For some time, various economic experts have asserted that we are moving toward becoming a service oriented economy, with few manufacturing jobs; that is the way it is, inevitable and we cannot change it. I took this to mean that in general, we should give up on the idea of manufacturing products in this country, and leave it to other countries to manufacture the goods we want and need, and then these countries would ship the goods back to the United States so that we can market and sell these products in the United States and elsewhere; again, for those countries that produced the goods? I often wondered how long that was going to last until some of those countries decided that they do not need the United States to serve as a middle-man and sell their products; they just need Americans to buy them. So, if this is the wave of the future, then in addition to losing manufacturing jobs, we now need fewer sales people.

COMPUTER TECHNOLOGY AND OUTSOURCING

The area of technology that I was a part of when there was a job boom, eventually slowed and the manufacturers of the hardware; the chips, computer boards, and other equipment that was once manufactured in the United States started leaving the country to reduce their labor costs.

Over the last decade or so, white collar jobs or jobs that produce the software to run on the computer hardware, have also left for those places where the labor is cheaper, or some would claim for the sake of productivity increases. Depending on the level of the business knowledge required to produce effective designs and program code, it can take a relative short time or even years in some situations for the outsourced resources to become productive. It often requires much effort on the part of domestic workers in the target area to make it a success. Training someone to take over your job does not sound appealing to me; does it to you? Many Americans have faced this dilemma.

From my own observations and prejudices, I am fairly certain that in many cases if these companies invested a quarter of the effort on training domestic resources, maybe even some college graduates, they would have seen productivity increases much, much, faster. At times, I have wondered if it is truly about productivity increases as these are numbers that can be tracked, compared, and reviewed; even revised when necessary to support a stated goal. Could it be that in some cases, company executives hear about the latest trend in something and feel the need to follow that trend; sound idea or not, as in the herd mentality?

IN SOURCING

To be fair, it must be acknowledged that our country is also on the receiving end of outsourcing in some industries. Several foreign automobile manufacturers have opened assembly plants in the United States. It is good business to do so, since we purchase many vehicles from foreign automotive companies. Plus, in recent years wages in some countries have risen, transportation and shipping costs have increased and the American worker is as productive as any other worker, so having their cars manufactured in America makes good economic sense. As a reminder, American car manufacturers also build cars in many other countries and for many of the same reasons; if people in these countries buy American cars, then why not build some of them there. My point is that this seems to work well within the automotive industry; why can't it work for most other industries?

HIGH TECH—CHIPS & PARTS

Recently, I heard stories on several national news channels, where some computer chips used in some of our military equipment was failing. They also discussed the potential impact to other industries in America that also used these bad computer chips. The gist of the story was questioning, why are we buying computer chips from a potential adversary; China. If I remember correctly, it was a company setup in America and that they bought the chips from a vendor in China and were now working with the vendor to improve the quality. Additionally, as a result of this problem, the government was going to improve their product review methodology and systems to ensure they checked future computer chips to ensure they are good, before using them. After awhile the story subsided and I never heard anything further on this matter. It did make me wonder whether China is the only country that is making computer chips and computer parts these days; what about Taiwan, Japan, South Korea, or the how about the United States?

I also remembered seeing reports that after the devastating earthquake Japan suffered in the summer of 2011, there was much concern about not being able to receive some auto parts from them and the impact it would have on completing assembly of many automotive cars, in the United States. I actually became aware of this before hearing it on the national news. At one time, there were hundreds of new cars parked in a local malls parking lot, or what used to be a thriving shopping area. I inquired about this and found out that these cars were awaiting parts from Japan before completing their assembly, and shipping them off to be sold. I realize we are in a global economy but I cannot believe we do not have a backup plan for these situations where we cannot obtain key parts for a product, or system; especially if it is part of our defense systems, when the source is unable or potentially some day, unwilling to provide them.

Backup Plan—Just in Case

As a world leader, I believe there are some industries and technologies that we should operate and manufacture in the United States to some extent, just for security reasons. If not even in a production mode, shouldn't we at least have the capability to quickly ramp up manufacturing facilities in case we need to?

We also have the capacity to become energy independent and in so doing, keep our energy costs lower than many other countries. This alone would help level the cost of production in the United States, and provide our manufacturers with the ability to afford higher wages and yet, still compete effectively on an international basis.

Quick Review of the Past

Our nation has been through a lot of booms and bust, in one industry or another, and we always seem to come up with something else to keep the economy moving forward. But, I think one trend that has been occurring over several decades, is that we are becoming less able to respond to these cycles as quickly as we once did. As more good jobs in the manufacturing industry, and others too, disappear there are correspondingly more unemployed. Additionally, I think we could be losing some skill sets that over time are not easily replaced. As a country, we could place ourselves in a real bind over a period of time as a result of those lost skills. Maybe we already have?

As a hypothetical example, what do we do if there comes a day when we need to start producing a product(s) like we used to do but no longer can, because we no longer have the skilled workers? I do not have an answer; however, I am sure some experts would say it is nothing to worry about in today's world. They might say, yes, these skilled workers that we need are gone, however, we can take some comfort in the knowledge that we can always get what we need from some other country; might be costly but still obtainable. Although this is just a hypothetical situation we might find ourselves in at some point, having to rely on another country to produce a product that we once did, does not comfort me; seems so unnecessary. As a country, I think it would be worthwhile to think about all this a lot more than we do; maybe even take a look at other cultures and countries, where they are now and where they once were. I have come to the conclusion that history is a window to the future. Hopefully, we can learn from the past.

There are some countries that to me seem to plan and cultivate their manufacturing capabilities a little more than we do; like Germany and Japan, even South Korea. Maybe we can learn something from them. Germany and Japan are both known for manufacturing and producing high quality vehicles, and technologically advanced devices. China is attempting to do the same with their industries.

Germany and Japan, had their industries and cities rebuilt after World War II, because they were obliterated during the war. In fact many countries were destroyed as a result of World War II, in one form or another, except for those primarily in North and South America. I remember my dad, a WWII veteran who spent a lot of time in Europe, complaining about us fixing them up (the Marshal Plan) after the war and that consequently they had better industrial equipment than did the United States; newer steel mills, state of the art factories, and so forth. Of course, he was looking and speaking at it from one point of view and not so much as saving Western Europe, Asia, and other countries from moving to communism. I think the Marshal Plan worked as designed, and today, I do not think we have to be overly worried about these countries moving to communism.

Another industry that has had its ups and downs is agriculture. Many years prior to World War II, many farmers and ranchers went through an especially rough patch too. My parents lived through this period and mentioned it from time to time. My dad grew up in Kansas so he had a ringside seat. The plains were especially hard hit with the draught that went on for almost a decade; in fact, some people refer to it as the dirty thirties. The famous author, John Steinbeck wrote about it in his novel, "The Grapes of Wrath". Through the infamous dust bowl and the lengthy depression, those in government, education, and in the private sector, worked together to do what they could do about stabilizing farm land and increasing their production. They also worked with farmers in terms of optimizing crop planning and rotation, and soil erosion preventative measures.

Improvements in technology removed the necessity for large numbers of laborers in the fields for most crops, but it created jobs too. John Deere is a household name and not only in the United States. Today, they and other manufacturers create and export farm equipment all over the world. Vast improvements in seeds, fertilizers and pesticides have boosted harvests tremendously and created high paying jobs. Almost everyone is aware that the industry still receives subsidies and that there have been financial crisis within the industry over the years, but on the whole it works well. We export our agriculture products worldwide. This has created many jobs related to just the exporting of these agricultural products around the world. Some examples of these jobs would be; buyers and sellers of the commodities on financial exchanges, storage facilities, and shippers (trucks, freight trains, and ships).

The agriculture industry is one of the more successful industries we have today in America; it is hard to outsource too. It does not hurt that we have some great natural resources like good land and water, but you know we have many natural resources that once went into making materials for other industries too; still could.

ECONOMIC COMPETITION—NATIONAL PROJECTS

Sometimes, economic competition and pressure from other countries, especially adversaries, have spurred our growth in one industry or another. For example, our nation did not get focused and energetic about the Space Program until the Russians launched Sputnik, into orbit around the earth, in October, 1957. Our leaders and the nation realized we were behind in the space race and needed to catch up with the Russians quickly. At the time we had several organizations in the military and public sectors that were working on rocketry and space exploration. NASA was officially created in October of 1958 and absorbed many of these organizations so that a coordinated and expedited effort could be put forth to win the race. We did not want a country, especially, an adversary that we were fighting a "cold war" with, sending satellites over our county without us being able to return the favor.

Once the space program got heated up, a ripple affect occurred with respect to new technologies and new jobs. New businesses began to spring up that supported the space effort. We began to associate products with the space program too. Many would identify Tang as being created by the space program, although, it was actually developed by inventor William Mitchell in 1957. He was working for the General Foods Corporation. NASA selected it to make the water in the life support system taste better and first used it in the Mercury program beginning with John Glenn's flight and later in the Gemini program. NASA did not invent Tang, but it did make it famous. It also created many new devices and technologies. One that I use around the house occasionally is the cordless power tool. In addition to creating new devices, they made improvements to existing devices and systems that are used in everyday life. If interested in additional examples, read more about them on the NASA spinoff sheet at website, http://www.nasa.gov/centers/kennedy/news/facts/ksc/nasaspinoff.html.

It should be noted that a lot of the technical knowledge and experience we utilized early in our rocket and space program was imported. Our government was smart enough to extract all the related technical information and scientific expertise from Germany (at the time they were the experts in rocketry and jet propulsion) at the end of World War II, that was available; and so did the Russians.

Another important project in our nation's history is the interstate highway system. Many people, including historians, believe it is the Greatest Public Works Project in our History. When driving on the interstate highways in some states, you might see a sign that says the Eisenhower Interstate System, and it might lead you as it did me to believe, that it was conceived by President Eisenhower, or at least started during his administration. However, this would be incorrect, according to the frequently asked question (FAQ) section from the Department of Transportation's website, http://www.fhwa.dot.gov/interstate/faq. htm#question1. It basically says that the idea for the interstate system was initially mentioned in Congressional documents in 1939, and received designations and approvals under various Federal-Aid-Highway Act's, throughout the 1940's. It further states that although he may not have conceived the idea, he fully supported the Act of 1956, which established the program and provided funding sources for it too. The first federal tax on gasoline was established in the 1930's and was 1 cent. To fund the interstate highway system, the federal fuel tax on each gallon of gasoline was initially established at 3 cents; it is now 18.4 cents. On top of each gallon of gas, states and some localities within states levy their own tax. For a look at what your state's gasoline tax is reference this website: http://www.commonsensejunction.com/notes/ gas-tax-rate.html.

With President Eisenhower's support of the national highway system, it really got moving in the 1950's and work on it continues today. President Eisenhower was the Supreme Allied Command in Europe during World War II, and I believe his having seen the German highway system, the Autobahn, a system they already had in place prior to World War II, surely helped convince him and others of how important the establishment of a National Highway System would be. He realized early on that as a major power, we needed this project to support our National Security interests and expand our economic capabilities, including employment. President Eisenhower served two terms in office and he and many historians, consider this as one of his most important achievements!

There are many sectors in the manufacturing industry that have been on a downhill slide for decades; some may not even exist any longer. I think we need to get past the point of arguing about whose fault it is and do something about it. We do not have to be the number one manufacturer in every product category in the world; it is probably better all around if we are not. There is plenty of room for good old fashion and honest competition. We have been here before; an example is our automotive industry. If you are old enough to remember, would you not agree that competition has improved the products our automotive industry produces these days? At one time, Japanese manufactured cars were considered a laughing matter?

However, overtime they kept improving their car designs and their quality and became a force to reckon with. While at the same time our manufacturers did not, and then all of sudden American made cars were not the hot ticket item. Many American consumers upset with the quality of American cars during this time period switched to foreign manufactured cars, and some still will not look at anything else today. That is unfortunate because American manufactured cars built today, are among the highest quality cars made anywhere in the world and the price is right on a lot of these American built cars and trucks.

There will always be some countries we have to compete with that use unfair trading practices, such as dumping of goods and materials below cost, and some that use illegal labor forces to dominate a market. There are methods to address those issues. We live in and compete with other members of the global economy. Our businesses export products to other countries and we import products from them. It is called international trading and it has been going on for a long time. It is a good system and people all over the world benefit from it. Competition is good. I believe it helps keep the peace too. Let us get back in the game!

The American National Transportation System (ANTS) will help bring a wide range of manufacturing back to America. Yes, we have manufacturing occurring in America today; it is just that we do not have enough. If we did then we would not be talking about the unemployment problem all the time.

IDEA's and Opinions

As to how this idea of the ANTS project came to me, I think it started years ago, when I was traveling down Interstate 70, heading East toward the University of Missouri, in Columbia, Missouri, from my home in Kansas City, Missouri, and of course, slowed to a stop. On the return trip, the same situation occurred. Only this time, we were moving, albeit it slowly moving but better than a complete stop; and while moving, I noticed a Department of Transportation (MO-DOT) sign that said, "If you have any ideas on how to fix I-70, please send them". Well at the time I must have been thinking about some ideas, but did not offer any suggestions. But I believe a seed had been planted.

More recently though, I believe the catalyst for the ANTS project started early in the summer of 2011, while working in my garden. I had removed a large ant hill that was in an ideal location for a tomato plant. Later on I noticed the ants were rebuilding the ant hill. In fact, over a short period of time, they had rebuilt that ant hill in another location and out of my way.

I somehow put this together with what I saw while driving to the city one evening for some relaxation time at the Kansas City Power and Light district; I noticed several aircraft fuselages (minus the wings) sitting atop railroad platforms as I drove along the highway and believe I got the first thought of high speed trains (HST) at that time. I gathered they were being delivered for assembly somewhere in the United States, but maybe elsewhere. I had really never thought about these high speed railroads before and then after some time of viewing all those television business and news programs constantly discussing the unemployment crisis, lack of an energy policy, and so forth, this idea of a multiuse platform came to me. After I began my research for this project, I learned that high speed rail has existed for a long time in other countries, and that our country is so far behind in this industry, it is not at all funny!

I began thinking about how early on in our country's history; we seemed to get things done one way or another. We expanded our agriculture capability and capacities by inventing new machinery to plant and harvest our crops, built factories and railroads, sold our products all over the world, made inventions for creating and harnessing electricity, and then devices to use electricity, like the light bulb and electric motors; created new processes like the assembly line, created transportation channels that sometimes seemed impossible at the time to do like the Erie Canal, the transcontinental railroad, and the Panama Canal.

As we moved into the twentieth century, our country expanded, grew and matured. Many of the inventions and devices we use today had their origin in earlier years; however, in the twentieth century they became useable and eventually common parts of our everyday life. There are so many, but a few examples are; commercial air conditioning, air transportation, transistors and solid state components. Radio and television became fixtures in the home and we rely on them for much of our news and entertainment. Atomic energy was harnessed. Cannot forget about the space program though; it thrilled us all and got us to the moon. There were many advances in the field of medicine too!

So what have we done lately, and what will we do in the 21st century? I hope a lot more. Americans are problem solvers by nature. We are not always the inventors but we do get things done when we want or need to. We improve things and figure out how to use new ideas and discoveries. What are we missing in America today?

We need leaders now; from the private and public sector to get this country moving forward! We have a huge problem; it is called Unemployment and it needs to be fixed. I believe this American National Transportation System would be a good launching platform for doing just that.

ENVIRONMENTAL CONCERNS

If you are an environmentalist this project is for you. It reduces the amount of impact on the environment that three separate systems would have, by combining them into one, and provides design capabilities to work around sensitive inhabitations, and leave a smaller footprint on the environment.

I consider myself an environmentalist too and have for many years. One of my favorite hobbies is gardening, vegetable gardening for the most part. I even recycle leaves into my garden along with other organic materials that most would discard and I rarely use any chemicals in it. I think I have been an environmentalist since I was a boy.

When I was a young boy, we used to fish with trot lines on the Kansas (Kaw) River. It was some work, but it was fun and occasionally provided some additional food for us. When we ran the lines and there was nothing on them it was not so much fun. At those times, I would always mention that we should fish a different spot, maybe even across the river, and my dad would ignore me. As you came down to the river bank in the light of day, you could see across the river and I always noticed a beautiful green pond close to the river bank on the other side and I wished we could go over there and fish. For some reason, the other side always looked better than where were fishing from and of course I often mentioned this point to my Dad, when fishing was slow. However, my Dad always argued that it was too far away and was not a better spot than where we were fishing. I knew better though.

Several years later, when I was a teenager and owned my own car I went over to the other side of that river to check out the pond that I had always dreamed of fishing in and sure enough; it was a lot further to get to. I had to drive down a long dirt road that went behind this factory just to get to the road that ran along the river and up to the pond.

As I drove along the road I noticed a creek that ran from the plant toward the pond and on to the river. It was cool looking and when I finally got closer to that pond, I was taken with the green looking water and could not wait to go fishing! Once I got out of my car and walked to the edge I realized that the pond was clearly not for fishing. It was for cooling the waste from the plant that made detergent and other laundry products and the pond even seemed to be bubbling in spots. After a few minutes the smell was becoming too strong to hang around, so I sighed and got in my car and left. Before leaving, I took a glance across the river and thought, hey that looks a lot better over on that side. I quit fishing in that river and a few years later, read where they were cleaning it up. Later, I encountered someone who had worked at that factory and learned it no longer was in use. He told me that that the company had opened a factory in Mexico, and closed the one by the river down.

My city has a recycle program and we participate in it fully. I believe the majority of Americans appreciate the efforts of environmentalists to keep the air, water and land free from pollutants and mass destruction. I also believe most people favor using renewable resources too if they can be economically justified to use now or in the near term.

This project provides the capability to collect and economically transport those renewable energies and bring them to consumers. We need to continue to develop and improve technology and implement that technology that will help our existing energy producers use their fuel sources cleanly and efficiently. Over the years, good progress has been achieved in cleaning up our environment and preventing pollution, and more is needed, but this does take time and money.

I believe our country needs to be energy independent and needs good jobs too. If we do not have both, then one day the last thing people will be worried about is our environment. I hope we can all work together to ensure we do everything possible to keep on improving our environment while using common sense in those matters that arise, regarding energy creation, and distribution.

BALANCED BUDGET CONCERNS

If you are someone who believes our government should have a balanced budget, then this project will help! The number of direct and indirect jobs created by this project, along with the ripple effect that will generate additional jobs will help get us there. By reducing the number of poor and those dependent on government support to survive, the resulting cost savings will help too. Add in the additional revenue from the income taxes on individuals and businesses, plus revenue from the fees collected from the operating components of the ANTS project and it should be much easier to balance our budget. Of course at some point the growth rate of expenses has to be paired with the incoming amount of money. If this is not done then we can never balance the budget.

A FINAL THOUGHT

The American National Transportation System is not "make" work. It is very doable; it is not like the Space Program in the late 1950's and 1960's when the technology did not exist to put a man in space, let alone on the moon. This system can be done now as the technology exists; other countries have it as regards the ground transportation portion of ANTS, and I am confident our engineers can innovate and design any necessary equipment needed for the energy, communication and passenger components of the system.

The first five routes should all be well on their way to completion within five years from the starting date of construction; some sooner.

Meanwhile, design, planning and construction, should be in progress for the next routes.

Hopefully, politics will not be an issue with too many of our elected representatives in government, but if there is, we have the peaceful means to remove those individuals from office, and replace them with Americans who want to get our country back on the right track!

This project will directly create hundreds of thousands of jobs in the design, engineering, manufacturing and construction industries. New or original equipment manufacturers (OEM's) will be needed to design and create equipment to install and service the ANTS platform and components. The ripple effect from all these jobs could increase the overall job count to a couple of million workers.

The reduction in the number of people from the unemployed and under employed roles should significantly reduce the related federal and states expenditures for supporting these folks via Food Stamp and other relief programs. Withholding taxes for Social Security and Medicare programs will increase and shore up those funds. Federal, state, and where applicable, local income tax revenues will increase through the payroll taxes on the employed and provide government income to balance and manage their budgets without drastically cutting current programs. It should significantly impact the housing problem in a positive manner too.

Additionally, I believe this will be the foundation for new manufacturing in the United States and help us be competitive in international trade for decades. Keeping energy costs low will spur innovation in the high technology areas related to the three components of ANTS, and contribute to our National Identity and Security.

We need to get this project moving. Target dates need to be established for completing the milestones necessary to get ANTS built and operational. This project creates good JOBS!

ACKNOWLEDGEMENTS

Designers and Engineers: In advance to those professionals that will step forward, to correct any design issues with this system, add their own ingenuity and innovation to the design, and hopefully, support this project!

Leaders in Business and Government: Most people understand that one of the easiest things to do is to find or make up a reason to not do something. However, I still have hope and believe in the system we have, so I thank you in advance for seriously studying this project; cooperating with one another to make this project a reality, and for doing so in a timely way so that we can get our country back on track!

United States Government Workers: I would like to thank all those government workers who collect, format and publish data and information on related department websites, along with all the statistics I studied and used in this effort. Some numbers were easier to understand than others, but they are available on just about any subject one is interested in studying. Many websites are not only informative, and interesting, but some even have interactive facilities that help in understanding and learning.

Veterans: For all who have served and are serving, thank you for doing so.

APPENDIX A

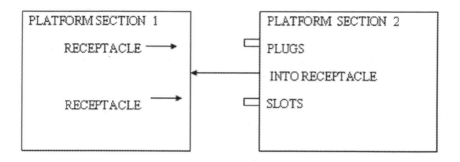

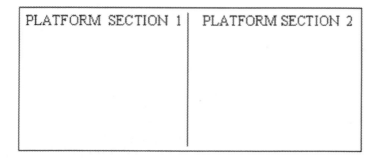

PLATFORM DESIGN FEATURES

Each standard platform will have extrusions at one end of the platform while the other end of the same platform piece, will have matching receptacles, so that one slot can be easily inserted (dock) into the previous platform to help align and strengthen the structure.

This illustration shows a surface view of two separate platform sections before and after construction.

A.N.T.S PLATFORM TYPE A: SURFACE VIEW

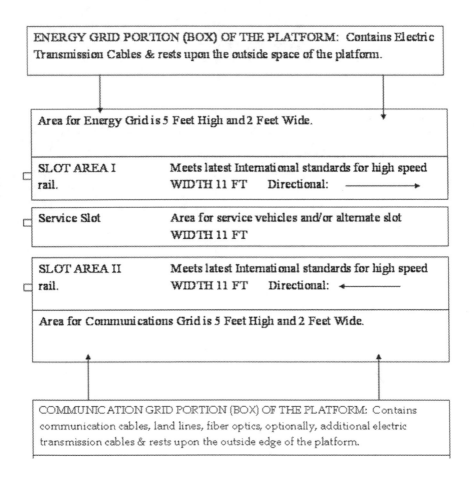

Notes:
WIDTH OF THE ANTS PLATFORM TYPE A IS 37 FEET.
STANDARD LENGTH OF PLATFORM IS 60 FEET.

A.N.T.S. Platform Cost Estimates

The following estimates are my estimates and values I used in their calculations were based on costs for materials used in constructing highways. These estimates do not include costs for construction of any bridges or facilities that the ANTS platforms would connect to at cities or along the routes, nor any material or equipment costs that the components would utilize as relates to energy, communications, or passenger transportation.

If interested in these estimates, a good source for these in your area might be your state department of transportation. Each state is responsible for the interstate highways in their own state including maintenance and enforcement of most regulations relating to its operation.

There are common factors that can increase the cost for construction of an interstate highway. These would include materials used, cost of the land, labor, terrain; does it cover long flat stretches of ground or is it in a hilly or mountainous area. Does it go through wetlands or require significant drainage control. Another concern might be the environment; is there a lot of excavation necessary and will the area disturbed around the interstate have to be landscaped.

For example, a mile of interstate highway could cost a half million dollars, or it could cost 5 million dollars; just depends on where it is located. ANTS, does not encounter some of these costs as the system is constructed above the grounds surface.

A.N.T.S. PLATFORM TYPE A:
COST ESTIMATES

TYPE A PLATFORM – LOWER COST ESTIMATE FOR MANUFACTURE AND
INSTALLATION for 500 MILES

DESCRIPTION	UNIT No.	UNIT COST	COST ESTIMATE
Platform Type A 60 ft prefab section	1	22800	$22,800.00
Support Pillars per 60 ft section	3	7600	$22,800.00
Installing One 60 ft section and supports	1	11400	$11,400.00
Cost - Manufacture and Installation 1 section	1		$57,000.00
Cost per mile (88 Platform Type A Sections)	88		$5,016,000.00
Number of miles on Route	500		
COST of Manufacture & Installation			$2,508,000,000.00

TYPE A PLATFORM – HIGHER COST ESTIMATE FOR MANUFACTURE AND
INSTALLATION for 500 MILES

DESCRIPTION	UNIT No.	UNIT COST	COST ESTIMATE
Platform Type A 60 ft prefab section	1	33000	$33,000.00
Support Pillars per 60 ft section	3	12000	$36,000.00
Installing One 60 ft section and supports	1	14600	$14,600.00
Cost - Manufacture and Installation 1 section	1		$83,600.00
Cost per mile (88 Platform Type A Sections)	88		$7,356,800.00
Number of miles on Route	500		
COST of Manufacture & Installation			$3,678,400,000.00

Note: These estimates do not include costs for design and engineering.

A.N.T.S. Platform Type B: Surface View

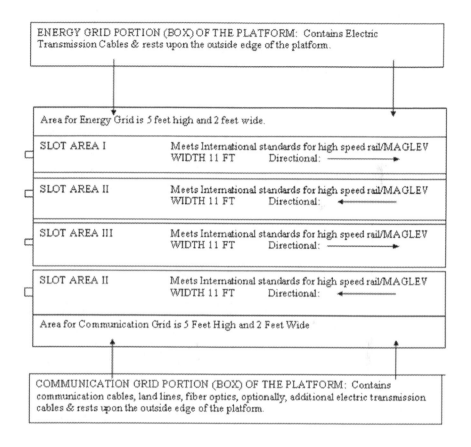

ENERGY GRID PORTION (BOX) OF THE PLATFORM: Contains Electric Transmission Cables & rests upon the outside edge of the platform.

Area for Energy Grid is 5 feet high and 2 feet wide.

SLOT AREA I — Meets International standards for high speed rail/MAGLEV WIDTH 11 FT — Directional: ⟶

SLOT AREA II — Meets International standards for high speed rail/MAGLEV WIDTH 11 FT — Directional: ⟵

SLOT AREA III — Meets International standards for high speed rail/MAGLEV WIDTH 11 FT — Directional: ⟶

SLOT AREA II — Meets International standards for high speed rail/MAGLEV WIDTH 11 FT — Directional: ⟵

Area for Communication Grid is 5 Feet High and 2 Feet Wide

COMMUNICATION GRID PORTION (BOX) OF THE PLATFORM: Contains communication cables, land lines, fiber optics, optionally, additional electric transmission cables & rests upon the outside edge of the platform.

NOTE: WIDTH OF THE ANTS PLATFORM **TYPE B** IS 50 FEET. STANDARD PLATFORM LENGTH IS 60 FEET.

A.N.T.S. PLATFORM TYPE B:
COST ESTIMATES

TYPE B PLATFORM – *LOWER* COST ESTIMATE FOR MANUFACTURE AND INSTALLATION for 500 MILES

DESCRIPTION	UNIT No.	UNIT COST	COST ESTIMATE
Platform Type B 60 ft prefab section	1	30000	$30,000.00
Support Pillars per 60 ft section	5	8000	$40,000.00
Installing One 60 ft section and supports	1	16400	$16,400.00
Cost - Manufacture and Installation 1 section	1		$86,400.00
Cost per mile (88 Platform Type B Sections)	88		$7,603,200.00
Number of miles on Route	500		
COST of Manufacture & Installation			$3,801,600,000.00

TYPE B PLATFORM – *HIGHER* COST ESTIMATE FOR MANUFACTURE AND INSTALLATION for 500 MILES

DESCRIPTION	UNIT No.	UNIT COST	COST ESTIMATE
Platform Type B 60 ft prefab section	1	46500	$46,500.00
Support Pillars per 60 ft section	5	12000	$60,000.00
Installing One 60 ft section and supports	1	19500	$19,500.00
Cost - Manufacture and Installation 1 section	1		$126,000.00
Cost per mile (88 Platform Type B Sections)	88		$11,088,000.00
Number of miles on Route	500		
COST of Manufacture & Installation			$5,544,000,000.00

Note: These estimates do not include costs for design and engineering.

APPENDIX B

INTERESTING FACTS

From cable television: History Channel show Modern Marvels: Copper and Gold are the only two natural metals with a unique color; all others are gray or white.

HISTORY OF DAMS FROM THE DEPARTMENT OF ENERGY:

http://www.eia.gov/kids/energy.cfm?page=hydropower_home-basics-k.cfm

Only a small percentage of all dams in the United States produce electricity. Most dams were constructed solely to provide irrigation and flood control.

Over half of U.S. hydroelectric capacity for electricity generation is concentrated in three States: Washington, California, and Oregon. Approximately 31% of the total U.S. hydropower is generated in Washington, the location of the Nation's largest hydroelectric facility—the Grand Coulee Dam.

Most hydropower is produced at large facilities built by the Federal Government, such as the Grand Coulee Dam. The West has most of the largest dams, but there are numerous smaller facilities operating around the country.

From Department of Energy: Website: http://www.eere.energy.gov/topics/water.html

American companies are developing innovative ways to generate energy from waves, currents, and tides. Currently, **hydropower** is the largest source of renewable electricity in the United States.

http://www1.eere.energy.gov/water/hydro_history.html

Humans have been harnessing water to perform work for thousands of years. The Greeks used water wheels for grinding wheat into flour more than 2,000 years ago. Besides grinding flour, the power of the water was used to saw wood and power textile mills and manufacturing plants.

For more than a century, the technology for using falling water to create hydroelectricity has existed. The evolution of the modern hydropower turbine began in the mid-1700s when a French hydraulic and military engineer, Bernard Forest de Bélidor wrote *Architecture Hydraulique*. In this four volume work, he described using a vertical-axis versus a horizontal-axis machine.

During the 1700s and 1800s, water turbine development continued. In 1880, a brush arc light dynamo driven by a water turbine was used to provide theatre and storefront lighting in Grand Rapids, Michigan; and in 1881, a brush dynamo connected to a turbine in a flour mill provided street lighting at Niagara Falls, New York. These two projects used *direct-current* technology.

Alternating current is used today. That breakthrough came when the electric generator was coupled to the turbine, which resulted in the world's, and the United States', first hydroelectric plant located in Appleton, Wisconsin, in 1882. (Read more about the Appleton hydroelectric power plant on the Library of Congress web page.)

B.C.	Hydropower used by the Greeks to turn water wheels for grinding wheat into flour, more than 2,000 years ago.
Mid-1770s	French hydraulic and military engineer Bernard Forest de Bélidor wrote *Architecture Hydraulique*, a four-volume work describing vertical- and horizontal-axis machines.

1775	U.S. Army Corps of Engineers founded, with establishment of Chief Engineer for the Continental Army.
1880	Michigan's Grand Rapids Electric Light and Power Company, generating electricity by dynamo belted to a water turbine at the Wolverine Chair Factory, lit up 16 brush-arc lamps.
1881	Niagara Falls city street lamps powered by hydropower.
1882	World's first hydroelectric power plant began operation on the Fox River in Appleton, Wisconsin.
1886	About 45 water-powered electric plants in the U.S. and Canada.
1887	San Bernardino, Ca., opens first hydroelectric plant in the west.
1889	Two hundred electric plants in the U.S. use waterpower for some or all generation.
1901	First Federal Water Power Act.
1902	Bureau of Reclamation established.
1907	Hydropower provided 15% of U.S. electrical generation.
1920	Hydropower provided 25% of U.S. electrical generation. Federal Power Act establishes Federal Power Commission authority to issue licenses for hydro development on public lands.
1933	Tennessee Valley Authority established.
1935	Federal Power Commission authority extended to all hydroelectric projects built by utilities engaged in interstate commerce.
1937	Bonneville Dam, first Federal dam, begins operation on the Columbia River. Bonneville Power Administration established.
1940	Hydropower provided 40% of electrical generation. Conventional capacity tripled in United States since 1920.

| 1980 | Conventional capacity nearly tripled in United States since 1940. |
| 2003 | About 10% of U.S. electricity comes from hydropower. Today, there is about 80,000 MW of conventional capacity and 18,000 MW of pumped storage. |

REFERENCES AND SELECTED INTERNET SITES

UNITED STATES GOVERNMENT WEBSITES:

http://www.house.gov/representatives: Good website to see who your representative is and what committees they are assigned, along with contact information.

http://www.senate.gov/: You can work around this site to find your senators and how to contact them; telephone, or via e-mail.

U.S. Department of Agriculture: http://www.usda.gov/wps/portal/usda/usdahome

U.S. Department of Commerce: http://www.commerce.gov/

U.S. Department of Energy: http://energy.gov/

U.S. Department of Homeland Security: http://www.dhs.gov/index.shtm

U.S. Department of Interior: http://www.doi.gov/index.cfm

U.S. Department of Labor: http://www.dol.gov/

U.S. Department of Transportation: http://www.dot.gov/

Federal Communications Commission: http://www.fcc.gov/

SPECIFIC ARTICLES/INFORMATION:

U.S. Department of Commerce—Statistics on U.S. Tourism **http://tinet.ita.doc.gov/outreachpages/download_data_table/2010_Key_Facts.pdf**

NASA Fact Sheet: http://www.nasa.gov/centers/kennedy/news/facts/ksc/nasaspinoff.html

Internet—General Again, much information available for source countries, international companies.

PROFESSIONAL ORGANIZATIONS

American Society of Civil Engineers: website, http://www.asce.org/
United States Chamber of Commerce: website, http://www.uschamber.
   com/

MEDIA SOURCES:

Background Information/Specific Information
ABC News Report—The Note: Congress Mulls Cuts to Food Stamps
   Program Amid Record Number of Recipients, by Huma Khan,
   website, http://abcnews.go.com/blogs/politics/2011/05/congress-
   mulls-cuts-to-food-stamps-program-amid-record-number-of-
   recipients/#comments

BUSINESS AND FINANCIAL NEWS:

Bloomberg Financial Network: Good source of business news,
   commentary, and investment information throughout the day and
   evening.
CNBC (Consumer News and Business Channel): Good source
   of business news, commentary, and investment information
   throughout the day, including the "Mad Money" show. Consumer
   reports in the evening; for example, the documentary on "The Race
   to Save American Infrastructure".
Fox Business Channel: Good source of business news, commentary,
   and investment information throughout the day; evening shows
   include: Your World with Neil Cavuto, and Lou Dobbs.

SELECTED NEWS & COMMENTARY:

Fox News Channel: The O'Reilly Factor, Hannity, On the Record with
   Greta Van Susteren
MSNBC: The Dylan Ratigan Show, Hardball with Chris Matthews,
   Politics Nation with the Reverend Al Sharpton

Websites By A.N.T.S. Components

Energy Component

American Electric Power Company—good website to get specifics on high voltage transmission systems and general information on all parts of the high voltage transmission systems, and alternatives to the high wire energy transmissions. http://www.aep.com/about/transmission/transmissionqa

Department of Energy—website provides about the 2011, National Environmental Policy Act (NEPA) with memorandums concerned with underwater energy cable use. http://energy.gov/sites/prod/files/nepapub/nepa_documents/RedDont/APS-2011-OE

Department of Energy—website for information relative to energy transmission http://energy.gov/transmission

Energy in brief website from U.S. Energy Information Administration. It is a good website for information on the electrical grid and related terminology. It also has links to good interactive and animated maps; see the power grid as an example. http://www.eia.gov/energy_in_brief/power_grid.cfm

Department of Energy—October 30, 2009 article: there is no "National power grid", there are actually three power grids, website, http://www.eia.gov/energy_in_brief/power_grid.cfm

Department of Interior—Study of Anthropogenic electromagnetic fields (EMF's) effects from undersea power cables on various marine life http://www.gomr.boemre.gov/PI/PDFImages/ESPIS/4/5115.pdf

North American Electric Reliability (NERC)—see mission statement, website: http://www.nerc.com/

Communication Component

The Federal Communication Commission is responsible for almost anything to do with communications by radio, television, wire, satellite and cable in all 50 states, the District of Columbia and U.S. territories. It was established by the Communications Act of 1934 and operates as an independent U.S. government agency overseen by Congress. http://www.fcc.gov/what-we-do

To see various communication networks visit this website and pick and
choose, particularly the USA National and Regional network maps.
http://www.telecomramblings.com/network-maps/

TRANSPORTATION COMPONENT

Federal and State Gasoline Taxes: http://www.commonsensejunction.
com/notes/gas-tax-rate.html

History of Federal Fuel Tax: http://www.fhwa.dot.gov/infrastructure/
gastax.cfm

High Speed Rail—Easy Access to plenty of information via most
internet search engines. Just search on the key words, for example,
high speed rail, MAGLEV

Associations of American Railroads: http://www.aar.org/

Department of Transportation: Go to the site and search on high speed
rail: http://www.dot.gov/

Federal Railroad Administration: Reports to Department of
Transportation: http://www.fra.dot.gov/

Federal Highway Administration: Reports to Department of
Transportation: http://www.fhwa.dot.gov/

History of American Railroads: http://memory.loc.gov/ammem/
gmdhtml/rrhtml/rrintro.html

Map of the United States Interstate Highway System: http://www.
onlineatlas.us/interstate-highways.htm

Map of the United States—Population Density: http://www.census.
gov/dmd/www/pdf/512popdn.pdf

GLOSSARY & TERMS

FAA: Federal Aviation Agency: reports to Department of Transportation.

FCC: Federal Communication Commission

FRA: Federal Railroad Agency: reports to Department of Transportation.

FWHA: Federal Highway Administration: reports to Department of Transportation.

Note: The following are my interpretations from the sources I have used in my research; local library, internet, television.

High Speed Rail: This refers to systems that carry passengers at high speeds and resembles traditional train systems in that the wheels ride on the rails. They can be powered by various means; gas turbine engines, electric powered engines where the source of power is overhead in the form of electric power lines. Check it out on the internet. It is amazing as to how far some countries are with these systems and how fast they can go.

HST: In general this is my terminology to represent High Speed Ground Transportation, which would be High Speed Rail, MAGLEV or other type of equipment operating on the Platform.

MAGLEV: Magnetic Levitation is a technology being tested and used in high speed passenger transportation. It uses magnetic fields installed in a slot or guide and the vehicle is suspended, no contact with the surface in the slot. Most do not consider this as a high speed rail as it does not ride on rails. It still transports people.

P3's: The three P's stand for Public, Private, and Partnerships. It's a contract between business and government and is one way for government to get work done, such as the toll road in Indiana that I referenced, without the government totally financing the project. The first I had heard of this was on the CNBC Special, "The Race to Save American Infrastructure". Of course, you can get additional details on various types of P3's on the internet or at some libraries.

Tie Line: As it relates to the energy component, it is a connection between electric power systems. In telecommunication systems it is often used to describe a communication channel for linking two or more points together.

War Bonds: In the United States, the government issued these bonds to help finance World War II, in addition to taxes.